FOR THE LOVE OF TREES...

IN PLYMOUTH AND BEYOND

Gloria Dixon and Andrew Young (Editors)
For the Love of Trees, in Plymouth and beyond

First published in Great Britain in 2022 by
Plymouth Tree Partnership,
Poole Farm, Plymouth,
PL6 8NF, England.

ISBN 978-1-3999-4084-9

Designed and printed by Bretonside Copy,
Mayflower House, 50-54 Bretonside, Plymouth PL4 0AU

Cover photograph by Younger Photography, Plymouth shows a salt-laden
Monterey pine on Plymouth Hoe with Smeaton's Tower behind.

Papers used in the production of this book are made from wood pulp
originating from sustainably managed plantations.

This book is dedicated to people everywhere who are planting and caring for trees, especially volunteers in the national Tree Warden scheme. Without their commitment our world would be much poorer.

❧ CONTENTS ❧

Introduction 7

   Gloria's Story 8

   Andrew's Story 11

Chapter I: Trees and Us 15

   The Artist 16

   The Local Historian 20

   The Environment Portfolio Holder 24

   The Woodturner 26

   The PhD Researcher 28

   The Green Estate Manager 30

   The Tree Warden 32

   The Tree Officer 34

   The Landscape Architect 36

Chapter II: Trees with History 41

   If Trees could Talk 42

   The Old Tree 46

   Bramley Bounty 48

   A Wartime Survivor 52

   Marks in Barks of Love and Loss 54

   Elms of Old 56

   Going to Extremes 58

Chapter III: Hands Across the Sea...... 61

Peaceful Canopies, Trees and Greenspaces
of Plymouth, Michigan 62

A Gift from Plymouth, Michigan................. 66

Brewster Gardens, Plymouth, MA............. 68

The Weymouth Pine................................... 72

A Friendship Forged.................................. 74

Chapter IV: Our Trees 79

Cherry Aid.. 80

Our Beech Tree... 84

School Trees.. 88

Ham Woods.. 92

Coronation Avenue................................... 96

The Jubilee Row Project............................ 98

Chapter V: For the Love of Trees 101

Plymouth Pear Trees.................................102

The Tale of the Church Pew......................104

Would you use Wood 108

How old is old?...110

Pavement Plantings..................................114

Branching Out with Facts & Figures...........116

Stand and Stare..118

Food and Furniture...................................122

Reflections..124

The Authors & Artists............................127

❧ INTRODUCTION ❧

Forests are about wood and wildlife but trees are about people. In this book we explore the stories of interesting people and what drew them to trees. They all have an association with Plymouth, a city that overlooks a fine natural harbour where the English Channel begins to meet the Atlantic Ocean.

Plymouth may be defined by its maritime heritage but its tree heritage is just as important. Indeed, it was the oak woods in its river valleys where trees reach down to the high-water mark that made ship building possible.

We, the editors, start the book by sharing our tree stories and hope that they and the other contributors will take you on the next step of your tree journey. It is frequently said, but nonetheless remains true, that every journey starts with the first step.

❧ GLORIA'S STORY ❧

I cannot remember when I first realised how important trees were to me. Certainly as a small child, like most others, I'm sure, I used to love scrunching through the leaves in the park on an autumn day when we were walking the dog. Never really thinking about where they had come from or what was happening. My parents had always loved their garden, but we did not have trees, our plots were too small. I remember how I used to enjoy walking through St Budeaux Churchyard, marvelling at the old yew trees there, and yes, leaning against them for a stolen kiss from my husband to be! No real understanding of how magical and majestic trees were even then. It was not until 2003 when we moved back to Plymouth that I needed something to do to meet new people, start new hobbies. We lived really close to Mutley Park and Thorn Park, two of the best kept secrets in the city. I thought I knew Plymouth well, but these two green spaces had escaped my attention. Not so anymore. There was an advertisement in the local paper about wanting people to come forward and become volunteer Tree Wardens, which entailed being an extra pair of eyes and ears looking after a specific green space in your neighbourhood. Why not, I thought, and that was the real beginning of my understanding and love of trees. I have been a Tree Warden ever since and it has given me so much joy and fulfilment. I am not good at Tree ID even now, but to me it is not a matter of knowing a name but enjoying what you see before you. To admire the bark, how many different patterns there are within it, how many colours in the leaves, the fruits that they bear and the homes they provide for all the creatures, to say nothing of the beauty they give to our landscapes, their symmetry and their changes throughout the year. Nature at her best.

One of the first things I did as a Tree Warden was to help organise a tree planting in Mutley Park for the children at Hyde Park Infant

School who were celebrating 100 years since the school was founded. We had the whole school in the park, about 240 children, and they all helped to plant an ash tree, with the aid of a teaspoon of soil each, the tree was planted and after a dodgy start - the tree was vandalised - I am pleased to say, it recovered and is looking great, sixteen years on. It was so encouraging to see the children on their way home from school that summer, watering the tree with drink they hadn't finished at school. The Trust for conservation volunteers managed our local Tree Warden network and were always on hand with tools, assistance and general camaraderie. I then went on to join the Steering Group of the Plymouth Tree Partnership and became a Trustee for a few years. I took on the role of organising talks for the group which together with summer walks and visits kept us busy throughout the year. We were lucky enough to secure funding from the National Heritage Lottery Fund to produce a book, Plymouth's Favourite Trees. What fun we had doing that. We enlisted the help of the local newspaper to ask people to send in their favourite tree stories. We chose our favourites and with the help of a professional photographer and some interesting facts about the tree species, we had ourselves a book, which twelve years on is still selling and people remember and recognise. We even had book signing days in a couple of stores in the city centre and a reception at the then Astor Hotel to launch the book, kindly paid for by the owner of the hotel, Joseph Louei. The Lord Mayor and Lady Mayoress attended and afterwards planted a tree on the Hoe. The money that we raised from the sale of the books was used for a special scheme of planting trees in school grounds, mainly primary schools. This was a great project to carry out. Many children in the inner city schools had never had the opportunity of planting anything, not even the joy of getting muddy had been part of their upbringing, mainly as many of them lived in blocks of flats. The children took great delight in planting the trees and hedges almost as much as we did! It was so satisfying to return to the schools, and in the main, see how the trees had flourished. I can't recall how many schools we visited or indeed how many trees we planted, but it was a very rewarding exercise and continued for some years.

In 2012 we thought we should mark the occasion of Queen Elizabeth's Jubilee by planting not just one, but sixty trees in Central Park, one for each year of her reign. The avenue would be known as

Jubilee Row. We were given permission, and it must be said a lot of help in achieving this, by Plymouth City Council Parks Department. The first consideration though was how do we fund the project. Not to be defeated before we started, I ventured out armed with a briefcase and wearing my best suit and knocked on company doors asking for a donation of £150 to plant a tree. Before too long, we had raised £10,000. You can read more about this project in our chapter entitled Our Trees. Once again, it was a most rewarding project to be involved with, learning new skills beyond my wildest dreams, and all down to my love of trees.

Hardly a day passes without me feeling grateful to my forefathers for leaving such a legacy in the amazing array of trees all around, and feel in a small way that I too am achieving this by planting trees for the next few generations to enjoy.

Editor's Note: Sadly the ash tree planted by Hyde Park Primary succumbed to ash dieback disease and after a storm in 2022 many of its branches dropped to the ground. There was no option left but to fell the rest of the tree. The remaining stump has started to sprout new shoots and is beginning to look like a shrub. We will watch with interest to see what nature decides next.

❧ Andrew's Story ❧

I grew up in Surrey, one of Britain's most wooded counties, and in the 1950s and 1960s it was common to see large trees in suburban gardens quite close to houses. Most people could not have been troubled by the problems that trees can cause and, if there were complaints, they were not about fallen leaves. Council workmen with their brushes, shovels and hand carts made sure of that.

My bedroom overlooked a small copse and I used to love watching the trees silhouetted against the setting sun, often with their branches moving in the wind. They gave me a sense that there was a world beyond waiting to be discovered.

There were fewer opportunities to travel then and it became my main reason to enter the Navy as an engineering cadet in 1970. Tree encounters were unsurprisingly few during most of my career and sometimes memorable for the wrong reasons. A navigation exercise had to be repeated after I planned to use the right-hand edge of a mangrove swamp as a lead mark only to find that it had submerged at high tide. Acorns that I took to the windswept and treeless Falkland Islands had not grown into young oaks when I returned some years later.

My early love of trees must have been growing subconsciously all the time. In 1990, I was in Devonport Naval Base with its dreary industrial landscape fashioned by two centuries of supporting the fleet through the eras of sail and steam. It needed a face lift and I had a part in that. It led to a chance introduction to the 'Men of the Trees' which subsequently became the International Tree Foundation. The charity donated trees and helped to plant them in corners around the Naval Base; it's amazing how many sites can be found if you go looking for them. It made me realise how Plymouth and most other places in Britain had fallen well short of their tree potential and I became an ITF member.

11

Around the Millennium, when pressures of work and family life were easing, I attended an evening class which led to me passing the Royal Forestry Society's Certificate in Arboriculture. At the same time, I took over chairmanship of the local International Tree Foundation group. We offered to replace sixteen newly-planted trees that had died in a roadside verge and the Council readily accepted. However, the replacement trees also died as we had not realised that they would need to be watered! We planted another sixteen trees the following year and, with regular watering over several hot, dry summers, they managed to establish. The project showed that volunteers could have a part in shaping the city's treescape. More than that, they could see and do things that were beyond the reach of any local authority.

The idea of a partnership between Plymouth City Council and voluntary groups was sealed in 2003 when the Lord Mayor formally launched Plymouth Tree Partnership in the leafy setting of the stables at Saltram House and awarded certificates to the city's first eight Tree Wardens.

Funding grants meant that the partnership could employ a co-ordinator at first and, very quickly, another thirty Tree Wardens were enrolled. There were practical demonstrations and evening talks to give us the confidence and skills needed to make a positive contribution. There were also plenty of tree plantings and I first met Gloria and her grandson, Oliver, at one of them.

When the funding grants ran out in 2006, I thought that was going to be the end of it but others in the group persuaded me that we had created something of value and could continue as a self-managed Tree Warden network. For the next four years, we kept an eye on the trees already planted and made ourselves available to help others plant trees. Also, in 2006, I started a remote-learning course that led to a foundation degree in arboriculture.

Ambitions moved up a gear in 2010 when the Government announced a national tree planting programme to plant one million trees in urban areas with just £4 million of funding. By then, I knew it cost many times more than that to buy and plant a 'standard' tree so it was with some scepticism that I submitted a bid from Plymouth Tree Partnership. Luckily, Langage power station was being built at the time and they had a planning condition to fund tree planting in the local area. It meant everything came together, with Plymouth City Council providing the planting effort and volunteer Tree Wardens the aftercare. It was a five-year programme and it made me very happy to see spaces that had once been empty furnished with new trees.

Plymouth Tree Partnership became a registered charity in 2015 to help raise more money for local trees and its volunteers have continued to respond to tree planting requests. I once read that tree planting is more about people than about trees and I have come to recognise how true that is.

New faces, new ideas, old faces and old friends make tree planting a truly rewarding endeavour and the sight of young trees growing strongly because of it all is simply the sealing pleasure.

❧ CHAPTER I ❧

TREES AND US

What is it about trees that make so many of us stand and stare in wonderment at their beauty? Is it their age, their many textures and colours? Or is it their ability to cleanse the air that we breathe and house innumerable creatures. Read the fascinating stories that follow from people from all walks of life whose very being depends on trees.

❧ THE ARTIST ❧
KEVIN TOLE

I have been a full-time self-employed artist since 2015 when I was made redundant from the oil industry. I am Plymouth born and bred but have lived all over the world including twenty years based in Glasgow. I moved back to Plymouth in 2010 and have established my art practice here. My work revolves around abstract oil paintings which are predominantly concerned with my life on oil rigs. My second string is in large charcoal drawings, mostly of trees and I am a member of the national group, The Arborealists. The book *Plymouth's Favourite Trees* proved to be a great help in locating and identifying great and specimen trees in the Plymouth area some of which I had not known about.

My early work revolved around a group of trees on the cycle path at Yelverton, above Clearbrook where a beautiful beech, *Fagus sylvatica,* a twisted oak, *Quercus robur,* and a blasted ash, *Fraxinus excelsior,* grew together. I spent a year there making one A1 sized charcoal drawing each week through all weathers to document the change in my perception of the trees and how each of them changed through the seasons. It was also important to document the local environment through the year. I took some of the fallings from the trees to hand-make charcoal at home and use this in the drawings. Beech makes particularly good drawing charcoal; ash is also good but oak is generally inferior for the purpose.

The tree and drawing I want to talk about is the Widey Oak in Widey Woods. It can be easy to overlook this tree, especially in summer with others around, but once you have spotted it, you will never miss it again. It becomes like the 'Patrician Tree' of Widey Woods, even more so than the utterly superb Lucombe Oak which is just around the corner. I wanted to produce a drawing showing the magnificence of this tree, which is one of the oldest in the Plymouth area. There is a tale that Charles I reviewed the Royalist troops in the siege of Plymouth beneath its branches in 1644, which would make it possibly more than 500 years old.

To do the drawing properly and from the best aspect I had to wait until autumn but that gave me plenty of time to walk in the woods and do some preliminary work with small sketches. Realising the oak charcoal would not be good enough I resorted to using beech twigs from the nearest trees and charcoaled them. In the meantime I took a lot of photographs to try and capture an essence of the tree. Any number of drawings of the tree can be produced to achieve this together with finding the qualities which make the tree stand out. The character of the beautiful living thing has somehow to be captured. To this extent I knew where I wanted to present it from. This was below the tree on a narrow path through the grass rather than from the upper tarmac path. It has been pollarded at various times and has lost several branches both large and small and bears the attendant scars.

Drawing in the field can be fun and it can also be a misery, especially when the ground is cold. When it is wet it is almost impossible although I have had interesting effects from rain drops bouncing off the paper and redistributing charcoal dust. I was lucky in that the weather was good in March when I finally got round to making marks on paper.

The first day it looks like I didn't get much done. But it established the twist at the heart of the tree and started to suggest the bulk of the trunk.

The work gradually proceeded with the hand-made charcoal and charcoal pencils of various grades along with rubbers of various sorts. Trying to keep the white of the paper is always the hard part, and

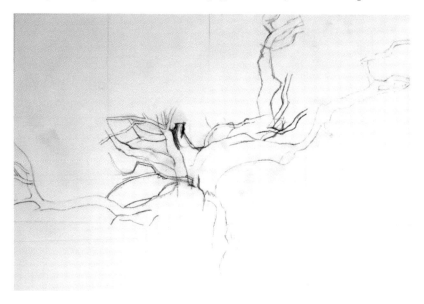

it is needed to form contrast, though I began to use white pastel (a misnomer as it commonly looks cream when compared to the paper). After three days I had the majority blocked in and a suggestion of the surrounding shrubs, small trees and fallen wood. What I had done, allowed me to return to the studio where I could work on the drawing and then return to the woods again when the need arose.

I got as far as the second picture below and headed out to do more work in the field to capture some more background. I ended up with the drawing to the right.

At this point I decided to leave it alone for a while and come back to it. There is a point when adding to a drawing can in fact detract from it. It needed time to work on me and to be able to look at it with fresh eyes.

That took about three months, and I feel I was right in leaving it alone. It could have stood, but the longer I looked at it the more I felt it missed something. So back on the wall it went and after another week I arrived here - less dark and more of the thin branches and twigs as well as a change in emphasis on the surrounds. Pleased with the result, I took it to the gallery where it looked good and drew much attention.

The finished drawing

❧ THE LOCAL HISTORIAN ❧
CHRIS ROBINSON

Back in 2008 a rather wonderful little book was published with the title *Plymouth's Favourite Trees*. As well as enjoying trying to spot how many of them you were already familiar with, and inspiring you to seek out those you weren't, it was also a great stimulus to start you thinking about your own favourite Plymouth tree.

Now I don't know about you but I have a number of favourites, and yes, a few of them were in there: the Copleston Oak at Tamerton, the great Widey Oak, and the Lucombe Oak in Widey Woods. To be honest I didn't even know that one had a specific name: I hadn't heard of Mr Lucombe before, however it really is a fantastic tree and puts me in mind of the great specimens Tolkien conjures up in his Ent world. Massive girth, a hollow in its trunk, huge sprawling branches, making it a worthy candidate for being one of the biggest, if not the biggest tree in the city.

However one of the other great features of the Favourite Tree book is to see the wide variety of trees we have on our doorstep, especially in some of the older parklands, like Saltram, Radford, Widey, Manadon and just across the water in Mount Edgcumbe. They all have such a fabulous range of trees, largely courtesy of their 18th century plant hunters who travelled the world to help their patrons have the finest and most diverse collection of species.

It was at Mount Edgcumbe that I saw a cork tree for the first time. I guess I'd never really thought about where cork came from before and I really was staggered to see what a cork tree looked like – amazing.

There are, of course, some excellent examples of splendid domestic trees as well, and one of my favourite tree collections is the wonderful array of palms that sit behind the red-tile-topped white wall of Sungates, that hacienda-like dwelling on the corner of Mannamead Road and Torr Lane, at the top of Hartley. Always makes me appreciate how lucky we are in this neck of the woods to have a climate in which such exotic plants are able to grow.

Perhaps one of Plymouth's hidden gems though, in tree terms, is the mighty mulberry in the Elizabethan Garden tucked away between

New Street and Castle Street on the Barbican. The planting here is essentially what you would have found in a garden in Elizabethan times, although I'm told the mulberry was little known in this country before the early 17th century, around the time the Mayflower spent a little time in the port.

As with all things however a favourite often comes on the back of a bit of historical baggage and for me it would be the very distinctive group of pine trees in Central Park, just below Pounds House. The house was built in 1829 by a wealthy local banker who was a keen sportsman. He is reputed to have buried his racehorses under the trees. As a schoolboy I have many fond memories of using two of those six trees as goalposts as my chums and I would aim to emulate our heroes, Geoff Hurst, Jimmy Greaves, Eusebio... Mike Bickle, whoever, and score great goals.

So when push comes to shove, probably my favourite tree today is the oak in our garden at home, because it gives me joy every day as I watch the leaves come and go through the seasons and marvel at how each year it seems happier, larger and more plentiful in its supply of acorns for those pesky squirrels.

Trees are great to draw and this is a sketch I did of the Six Trees in Central Park about 40 years ago! It features in my first book, *Plymouth As Time Draws On*, which in turn was based on a series of articles I was writing for the Herald back in the early 1980s.

Palms at Sungates, Torr Lane

Silver Maples, Frankfort Gate

THE ENVIRONMENT PORTFOLIO HOLDER
COUNCILLOR SUE DANN

I have always loved trees; in my small garden we have planted seven small trees plus four we have thriving in big pots. It means the value and the beauty of trees comes fresh to me every day. Being a Plymouth City Councillor and holding the portfolio of the environment brings responsibilities, and for me personally it has given me the joyous opportunity to make our city a greener place in which to live, work and play.

Having adopted the Plan for Trees in 2019, the city embarked on a new journey for managing trees. We had brought partners together to set out the objectives for promoting, protecting, caring for and enhancing trees across the city, and with that strong foundation we could move forward with confidence.

Lockdowns have, beyond doubt, shown how much people treasure green spaces. We have appreciated nature, and having constant access to our parks and nature reserves has really helped to improve our health and wellbeing. It has been a real opportunity to show how trees with their array of shapes and colours can benefit both place and people.

Climate change has also raised people's awareness about the importance of having trees in our communities and neighbourhoods and today there is a lot more understanding why trees are good for the environment. The need to plant more trees and celebrate our green spaces is a key part of the Plymouth Climate Emergency Action Plan. Tree planting has become a way of engaging with communities and people across the city with activities that reflect the climate change narrative.

Trees capture carbon improving air quality and reducing pollution. Their canopies give shade on hot summer days. They help reduce flooding, provide homes for wildlife and connect green spaces together. How pleasant it is to walk from one community to another through green corridors; we aim to provide more of these across our region. Living in a city, an urban built up environment, it is so important to include green spaces as the city grows. Trees do this; they soften a hard landscape and can bring a different use to a built-up space. So in my role as a portfolio holder, when looking at new tree planting and projects, my intention is to build back sustainably with greener canopy cover in some of Plymouth's inner city areas. This does depend on listening to what communities would like in their neighbourhoods, and being prepared to explain the issues.

The Tree Plan is all about informed planting, having the right tree in the right place. For some people, trees are like Marmite, you either love them or hate them. There is also the dichotomy of how the city builds and develops. There are always going to be occasions when people want to remove trees. The aim is to put back more than we take out, build back better and greener.

With funding from the Forestry Commission, matched by Plymouth City Council's investment programme, in 2020 the plan delivered nearly 2,500 new trees including 1000 standard sized trees. This represented a significant upscaling from previous years – about five times more than were planted in 2019 and 10 times more than the three previous years. Planting spots were identified by local people from all walks of life. A huge amount of administration followed behind the scenes as well as ordering stock and organising the planting schedule. In mid December the Green Estate and Street Services teams joined forces to plant the trees. This continued until the end of March, when all the trees were in the ground, a very creditable achievement.

The Tree Plan can't work miracles and there will always be areas for discussion, but I hope that the leadership shown in its development, and having a political advocate to promote the importance of the green agenda means that trees in Plymouth can only blossom and bear fruit.

ERIC ANNING

What is it about wood that makes it so attractive and tactile? Often at craft fairs folk will pick up the pieces on display, run their fingers over the surface and ask: "How did you make that?"

The story begins with the humble tree, this amazing structure which gives us a really useful material - wood - and for millennia humans have been using it as fuel and material for crafts and buildings.

As a woodturner I start with a log from a tree surgeon or, if the log has been processed in a sawmill, a plank of wood. The freshly felled timber is full of water so before it can be used it needs to be seasoned to prevent it from warping and cracking. Seasoning wood is a slow business as it takes about a year for every inch of thickness to air dry timber.

Sometimes woodturners deliberately use unseasoned wood to turn thin walled bowls and vases. The drying out process continues and changes the object from round to perhaps oval or a wavy edged shape; it might produce cracks and the end result can be pleasingly artistic rather than utilitarian, or it may be destined for firewood!

Selecting the type of timber from the huge variety available is the next step. Should it be softwood or hardwood, dark or light, highly figured or plain, newly felled or recycled? Much of the answer will depend on what is to be made, but unless it is recycled timber, it should always be from sustainable sources. Items such as chair or table legs, tool handles, stair spindles and newel posts generally need straight grained timber; utility bowls, platters, chopping boards, spoons and other culinary items and children's toys need a food safe timber; the highly figured and naturally coloured timber comes into its own for decorative bowls, boxes, vases, lamps and hollow vessels. One of the joys of decorative woodturning is to reveal the patterns, textures and colours laid down by the tree during its life.

People have been turning wood for thousands of years. The basic equipment of a lathe and a gouge or chisel is the same but there have been huge advances in the manufacture and type of equipment available. The choice can be daunting so a good way of finding out about the craft is to join a woodturning club like Plymouth Woodturners. There you will find a group of people keen to pass on their knowledge and help one another enjoy all aspects of this amazing hobby.

Like a lot of things woodturning is a fairly simple skill to learn. However to perfect the craft takes years of practice. My woodturning journey started in 1997 and I am still learning about ways of improving and honing those basic skills. During that time I have been guided by the few important rules in woodturning - work safely, protect yourself and others, keep your tools and your mind sharp but above all enjoy the experience.

A particular interest of mine is the challenge of making newel posts and stair spindles for old or listed building renovations. The originals may be a hundred or more years old. The process of visiting the site, taking measurements, making drawings and producing a newel post or a few spindles that look identical to the originals is most satisfying.

Turning the wood to the shape required is not necessarily the end of the process. The turned item can be enhanced by adding colour, carving a design or letters, texturing the surface, filling natural "faults" with resin or metal, even scorching with a blow torch. Once satisfied with the result the piece needs a protective finish.

Forming a shapeless lump of wood into a thing of beauty; working with hands, eyes and brain; devising shapes; actually producing something you can be proud of, is the beauty of woodturning.

Turned chair and bowl by Eric Anning

ALI NORTH

In each new town or city where I have lived, I have been quick to seek out the trees. The gnarly oaks, the billowing willows and the grand redwoods. This began when I lived in Cambridge. It was here that along with friends, fellow rock climbers and nature conservationists, we formed an urban tree-climbing club. When I moved to Plymouth in 2019 I was keen to embark on another urban quest - to find and document the most magnificent trees across the city. In an amazing act of serendipity I discovered the 2008 *Plymouth's Favourite Trees* book. This quickly became my guidebook as I cycled to unexplored green spaces, admiring their woody characters and reading the stories behind each one.

My pursuit of trees enabled me to find the wilder corners of Plymouth and I often found myself in places I didn't expect - behind a row of garages admiring a gnarly old sweet chestnut or at the pathway to a church, appreciating grand old elms framing its entrance. I started mapping new trees I encountered along the way, often climbing up into their branches and sketching my favourites; fully appreciating the twisted branches, the knotted bark and the impressive trunks towering into the sky.

When COVID hit we were largely confined to our houses. My radius for exploration significantly shrank and I soon became accustomed to the cemetery at the top of my street. An impressive copper beech standing tall in the centre quickly became my favourite tree in Plymouth. I'd listen to the crows chattering in its branches, admire the sun shining through its vibrant leaves and the crinkly lichen covering its bark. The leaves changed colour

Above: Copper Beech, Ford Park Cemetery
Below left: Ali doing what she loves best

throughout the summer, with the undersides gradually transitioning from bright copper to varying shades of green. Rounded knuckles were scattered up the trunk, presumably potential branches it had stopped investing growth in. For what has been a strange and stressful year, time spent admiring this tree brought a lot of comfort. I could clamber into its branches and sit in what seemed like a perfectly formed seat. From here I could see that the tree must have meant something to quite a few others in the past too. Notes and initials – difficult to read now that the bark had tried to heal itself - had been haphazardly engraved as a lasting memory.

Often it is the historical attractions that a newcomer will visit when arriving in a new town or city; monuments or listed buildings full of history. It is so often forgotten that there are ancient living structures lining park pathways, churchyards, cemeteries and allotments of every urban settlement across the UK. Wise old wooded giants, living through pivotal moments in history. I'm glad the copper beech was there to see me through 2020 - a year that will certainly be remembered for a long time to come.

CHRIS AVENT

As autumn descended in 2020 and we adjusted not only to the flow of the seasons but also the latest stage of COVID restrictions, a day leading work to evolve the green estate of Plymouth could never have been so challenging. As a society we are confronted with the reality of a rapidly changing climate, a rocky economic situation and a crisis in the health and wellbeing of a great many people. This has catalysed into a changing public perception and recognition of the importance of natural space as well as a willingness to change the way we think about it.

Personally I take great pride in being at the forefront of this evolution, working with many others who have a similar drive to protect our natural heritage and change the immediate future for the better.

My day to day activities can embrace an eclectic mix of tasks ranging from forensic work to understanding the financial realities of the city's green estate, building the skills requirements of the workforce, exciting project delivery such as understanding how to install an otter pass in a beaver fence and developing ways to support Friends Groups in our city's green spaces.

In terms of trees, the last two years have been like no other and all of this has been underpinned by the excellent foundation that the city's Plan for Trees has provided. The creation of this plan took two years of hard work and required a range of stakeholders including volunteer Tree Wardens. So much credit must go to all of those who took part. The Plan has provided a superb strategic platform which is recognised far beyond the boundaries of Plymouth and has brought much new funding into the city. It enabled over 1000 standard trees to be planted in 69 schemes across the city between October and March, all through the second wave of the pandemic. They included a Miyawaki forest to enhance a small area of rough ground in the St Budeaux area of Plymouth and it will be interesting to see how nature responds to this new opportunity.

My ambition does not end here though and there is still so much more to achieve despite new setbacks such as dealing with ash dieback

Miyawaki Forest, St. Budeaux, with the Brunel and Tamar bridges in the background

disease. It will need the continued dedication of people from all sectors and communities and there is every reason to see a really bright future. Although some days I still long for a day leading a tree planting event (and I do still make time for this) with the excitement of a group of young people realising that they have planted something which is likely to be alive when their grandchildren are old, I do appreciate the role that I have to facilitate the growth of a place on the planet where trees and the natural environment are recognised as an intrinsic part of where we live, giving enjoyment to generations to come.

Editors' Note: A Miyawaki Forest: Japanese botanist, Dr Akira Miyawaki pioneered a methodology of densely planting trees on small plots of land to quickly restore habitat and attract an abundance of wildlife. His 'tiny forests' have inspired conservationists everywhere.

❧ THE TREE WARDEN ❧
DAVID FROST

My lifetime interest in trees comes not only from their age, but also from their grace, their presence, and the way they quietly enhance our world. It always distresses me when seemingly thoughtless decisions are made to fell trees which apparently stand in the way of progress, with no thought to their age or right to be there.

My interest was re-awakened a few years ago when I attended a walk that highlighted some of the city's fine trees and it was amazing to learn about their life stories. Some were planted to commemorate historical events, such as the 350th anniversary of Mayflower's sailing in 1620, others to seal a connection with cities overseas, and others as part of a grand design for Plymouth after the war. I have lived in Plymouth for over 40 years, yet I had paid little heed to these majestic occupants of our city space! My eyes were opened! I joined the Plymouth Tree Partnership and became a volunteer Tree Warden.

In my chosen area I keep an eye on recently planted trees in case they need attention. I go out wearing a hi-viz vest to identify me as a volunteer and carrying secateurs and a bag for clippings. I am on a mission! Sometimes, there is sprouting growth at ground level which needs to be cut back to prevent it from becoming dominant. Tree support stakes may require attention too; they are essential when a tree is first planted but very often forgotten about as it grows. If left unchecked, they can rub into the bark and I have seen one tree literally growing around the stake! Sometimes I find tree ties cutting tightly into the bark and it is a very simple job to loosen or remove them.

Having attended some of the practical training courses run by the Plymouth Tree Partnership, I can put this knowledge to good use. People sometimes ask what I am doing so it is useful being able to explain how a tree grows and how

Below left and above: Plymouth Tree Partnership volunteers

tending it during its early years is really beneficial to the tree. I am providing an extra pair of eyes for the wellbeing of the tree.

Watering the newly planted trees is vital during the summer months to ensure they get a head start and literally a good footing into the ground. It is also a time to clear weeds and grass growing around the base of young trees and to add a mulch dressing if appropriate. Wood chippings are ideal for this and easily obtained from local tree surgeons wanting to avoid waste charges. Keeping a tree clear around its base not only helps it to grow but also makes it less likely to be damaged by careless grass cutting.

Plymouth's Tree Wardens have a monthly team session when we lend a hand in places where extra help is needed. The sessions are organised with the Council so piles of clippings, stakes or guards can be collected. There is often more than the boot of a car can take! By joining forces with friends of parks and like-minded people in community groups, we make a huge difference to the health of local trees and probably our own wellbeing too. It is so satisfying to see a young tree succeed and to know that it was only because we spent a few hours here and there doing some simple tasks in the fresh air.

It is also satisfying to know that, tree by tree, we are making a more attractive city and a better world for the future. A legacy in wood!

❧ THE TREE OFFICER ❧
JANE TURNER

The first thing to say is that no two days are the same, if you want a job that has variety and challenge this is the job for you!

I get to meet and work with a whole range of different characters and professions with the sole aim of trying to - in the words of the city's Plan for Trees - 'promote, protect, care and enhance trees in Plymouth'. In one day I can serve an emergency Tree Preservation Order (TPO); comment on a planning application; assess several applications for works to protected trees; prevent the felling of a tree; attend a meeting with partners to develop tree friendly planning policy and issue letters of enforcement in relation to illegal felling of trees.

It cannot be denied that some people do not like trees or are even fearful of them. A major challenge of the job is finding the time to convince them that their tree is not going to fall and damage their house, greenhouse, car, or shed, or that its roots are not going to block their drains. If they can see that their tree is an asset and not a liability, I feel my time has been well spent. It can be very trying, however, staying positive when, for the tenth time that day, you speak to someone who says they love trees, but… not the one in their garden that drops leaves on their patio, drops fruit on their car, casts shade and worst of all - dares to grow! Perhaps the most taxing cases are when neighbours are in dispute over a tree or a high hedge. They can be irate and I have to remain calm and impartial while listening to their claims and counter-claims.

Apart from the people aspects, there are many technical challenges. Perhaps the most satisfying is negotiating amendments to development site layouts so that important trees are retained and have space to thrive.

For whatever reason people come into contact with me, whether it is for permission to trim a tree, a request to make a TPO or to build a house, I want to help them take pleasure in the trees around them and see them in a positive light.

Working with colleagues in the city's planning department, we have the difficult task of achieving a balance between the requirements for much-needed new homes and infrastructure whilst at the same time

Silver Birch, Morlaix Drive, Derriford

protecting important trees and woodlands. Several of those woodlands are quite new having been planted by communities in the early 1990s. The foot-high whips then are now semi-mature woodlands helping our city breathe and providing a home for its wildlife and a place of reflection for its residents.

The competing demands of development and green space will continue and, as we know, trees do not always come out on top; but with robust policies in place and informed support from the community and their elected representatives, trees are being saved and even more new trees planted. This must be the way forward if we are to leave a city to be proud of for future generations to enjoy.

JAMES BROWN

I remember an occasion as a child of 3 or 4 when I was in the beautiful rock garden of my venerable great-aunt. As I paused in front of a compact Japanese Maple tree and looked through the leaves into the sky, I had an indescribable sense of the infinitude of the universe. Unable to digest this, I ran inside and tried to explain to the adults what I had experienced. But finding words inadequate, I resorted to bursting into tears!

Nonetheless, a sense of the magnificence of trees and the natural world has followed me since and was one of the reasons for re-training as a landscape architect. From memories of fissured pine tree trunks lit golden-orange in the sunset when growing up in a sandy enclave in Surrey, to the scrunchy autumn leaves of elms and oaks at school, and later, the unbelievably long strips of dangling bark suspended from giant mountain ash, *Eucalyptus regnans*, in the Dandenong ranges in Australia, I have marvelled at the wonder, stateliness and beauty of trees. The wider my experience, the greater my appreciation and enjoyment.

I have many favourite trees, with each year bringing another species or so to the fore of my attention. Where has it been all this time, I muse? This began when I lived in Australia and was mesmerised by the silver-blue willow-like leaves of Eucalyptus trees, rippling against the intense blue sky and contrasting with the rich ochre outback soil. Eucalyptus remains high in my arboreal affections, like an early love, and their unlikely and exuberant flowers which burst out from 'gum nuts', never fail to make me smile with delight. Years later, as a recently qualified chartered landscape architect, I recall noticing whitebeams in a London park, their felt-soft glaucous-green spring leaves making an eye catching contrast with the purple foliage of a nearby *Corylus avellana 'Purpurea'*. A spring walk to the valley gardens in Windsor Great Park brought the amelanchier to my notice. Its multi-stem incarnation has been a frequent choice of mine for its delicate white spring flowers, elegant foliage and autumn fiery tones.

Liquidambar was a surprise discovery in name and display. Its striking, elegant purple colour in autumn as it concludes its way through

Plane Tree in pencil by Sylvia Hofflund

yellows, golds and reds in a spectrum equivalent of shape shifting, made it a valued selection. It sits well beside and behind another wonderful find, the Persian Ironwood tree, *Parrotia persica*. They made a successful pairing at a residential retirement scheme in Slough, bringing together a blaze of complementary autumn colours. Around that time I was designing a large community park which I decided to flank with London planes. As a London resident then I had a 'thing' for plane trees, *Platanus x hispanica*, for their impact on streets, parks and wider landscapes. Their foliage is shiny green and resilient, their seed heads (known as 'dingleberries' by Californians) are spherical and spikey with stiff hairs, hanging like baubles, and their bark reminds me of giraffes' skin. What's more, on balmy summer evenings, they emit an exotic, if low key, scent of balm. I have not found that corroborated in any literature, but I am absolutely convinced!

Mulberry, *Morus nigra*, is a joyous tree. The trunk is characterfully gnarled, even on an immature tree. Fruits are large, juicy and wickedly staining! There is no cunning feasting on the late summer berries, (ripe when red turns to purple), without a tell-tale record on lips and fingers... and probably shirt, for that matter! Best not to plant close to anything

37

where the digestive outcome of hungry birds may cause an issue, as the colour, (and the staining), of the fruit pass right through. When I worked as a landscape gardener in London, it was a joy to climb a mature mulberry tree in St Johns Wood and pick the fruit for a wealthy client, not for them to eat, but their expensive car was parked nearby, whose white paint they wished to maintain without fruity blemish!

I think an overlooked tree is the humble hawthorn, *Crataegus monogyna*. It provides great value as a living sculpture, bending and twisting with the wind to form dramatic poses. Its late-spring abundant blossom being the harbinger of warmer days to come, it shares a gently sweet, but earthy aroma that lingers discreetly within its immediate environs. I liberated a potted specimen from years of confinement when I moved from a London flat to a house with a garden in Plymouth, and was rewarded with frothy cascades of off-white blossoms. This has been accentuated by pruning it to the shape of a palm tree. In early May, in full regalia, it looks like a creamy, floral umbrella.

I value trees for the character they bring in defining a 'sense of place'. Their scale, texture, colour, form and above all their natural quality, are essential counterpoints to man-made creations: buildings, roads, and grey infrastructure. I note that planting trees is much more talked about now, reflecting concern over climate change and an emerging awareness of nature's benefits to our wellbeing and health. Yet as a landscape designer, it is surprising how much reluctance there has been over many years by developers, local authorities, government, and design professionals, (landscape architects excepted!) to enable and encourage tree planting. I hope that the contributions to biodiversity, ecosystem services, wonder and beauty that trees provide, can be increasingly appreciated and enjoyed by everyone so that we ask: "Why don't we have a tree/trees, here"... in this garden, street, green space, town square, business frontage, school yard, hospital, field?

An experience that was moving and sobering in equal measure was visiting the much declined stands of Redwoods, *Sequoia sempervirens*, in California. Once the standard coastal tree that thrived in the misty onshore breezes, it is now reduced to small pockets in National Parks. Standing at the base of an older specimen, the trunk spongey-barked, fibrous and rusty coloured, I lifted my head to look upward and follow the tree's ascent. The sheer scale of it made me draw breath, exhale slowly and marvel. And then I felt a deep sadness for the enormous loss of the great forests of old. It is an arboreal equivalent to the decimation of the rhino or the bison herds. The same has occurred in New Zealand with the Kauri forests, great thick stemmed trees that seem to rise forever, and make one realise how small we are; how there is this bigger thing at play: nature. And although we fail to fully understand its systems, processes and gifts, we impact it without properly knowing and comprehending the consequences.

I have a recollection from Kerala, India, in the late 1990s, which for me is an example of the practical and aesthetic value of trees. Newly arrived, nothing prepared me for the richness and depth of colour of the dark green palm trees, which decked the vibrant orange-red soil. Riding in a rickshaw, I was spellbound by the dawn sunlight piercing through gaps in the palm trees beside the narrow road and illuminating, in theatrical effect, the mist that lingered around the forest edges. The trees gave shade to people and animals from the hot sun, and their fronds comprised the thatch roofing for the clusters of mud brick homes, demonstrating a wonderful economy of form and function, utility and grace. This experience is one of my strongest memories, and was put into poetic context later, when shared with an elderly Indian man, who replied, "Trees are earth's endless effort to reach the listening heaven", (Kochi).

Fruit of Mulberry Tree

39

❦ CHAPTER II ❧

TREES WITH HISTORY

History is laid down, layer by layer, in each successive year. So it is with trees. The changes are mostly imperceptible but sometimes there comes an event with great commotion; a dagger is drawn, a bomb explodes, a land is discovered or a seed is planted. In every case they work together to tell a story that is interwoven with human and arboreal interest. Some of those stories are told here.

❧ If Trees could Talk ❧

by Paul Copleston

People call me the Copleston Oak because beneath my branches Christopher Copleston murdered his godson on the 22nd day of March 1562. Although hollow and shrunken now, I stand in the same place outside St Mary's Parish Church in the village of Tamerton Foliot, Plymouth, and can still picture the scene on that fateful day.

The godson was Christopher Monns or Monnes, and some say he was an illegitimate son of Copleston. He had been sent abroad for his education and when he returned home, he overheard his godfather's conversation and repeated it amongst his circle of friends, which action soon found its way back to his godfather who was exceedingly angry. He resolved to make the boy pay for his actions.

They next met at a church service at St Mary's and when the godson saw the angry look on Copleston's face, he fled before the service had ended. His godfather fooled the lad by telling him that they could meet at church the following week as his anger had dissipated. The godson went to church and again left before the end of the service, carrying a sword and shield in his hands. Seeing this, Copleston ran after him. They exchanged abusive language before Copleston struck his godson below his left shoulder with a dagger, killing him instantly. Copleston immediately fled and went into hiding.

Copleston was well known at the court of Queen Elizabeth I and she pardoned him from the gallows, although he had to forfeit many of his Cornish properties in order to pay the hefty fine imposed on him. However, these forfeited manors were all quickly returned to Copleston and two years later he was made a Justice of the Peace!

The original pardon is held in the Public Record Office at Kew. It was written in Latin and contains a great deal of repetition, so this is only a summary:

The Queen to all to whom these presents shall come, greeting. Whereas Christopher Copleston formerly of Warleighe in the County of Devon, esquire, was indicted at a certain inquest previously held at Tamerton Folyett in the County aforesaid on the 22nd day of May in the 4th year of our reign (1562) before our coroners in the County of

Copleston Oak, Tamerton Foliot

Devon, on the sight of the body of a certain Christopher Monns alias Monnes, formerly of Wolston in the County of Cornwall, yeoman, lying dead at Tamerton Folyett, because the aforesaid Christopher Copleston on the 22nd day of March between the hours of 10 and 11 before noon of the same day was in a certain place there known as the Towne place alias Canne greyne, when an argument arose then and

there between the aforesaid Christopher C. with abusive language and taunts between Christopher C. and Christopher M. At that moment Christopher C. violently, that is to say, with a certain small weapon known as a dagger, worth four shillings, which the same Christopher C. was carrying in his right hand, held it into the said Christopher M. who was standing there with a sword and shield in his hands. He (Christopher C.) insulted him and with this small weapon suddenly and feloniously struck the aforesaid Christopher M. below his left shoulder, giving him a certain fatal wound six inches in depth and one inch wide, from which wound the same Christopher M. instantly died, an act contrary to our peace, our crown and dignity.

Be it known that by our special grace and from our certain knowledge and of our own motion we have pardoned, released and discharged and by these presents for us, our heirs and successors, we do pardon, release and discharge the said Christopher C. formerly of Warleighe in the County of Devon Esq. or by whatever other name the same Christopher C. is distinguished, known, called or named, from the aforesaid crime, homicide and killing of the same Christopher M.

Christopher Copleston, who was spared the gallows in 1562, was my 11th great uncle, and every time I pass the oak tree outside St Mary's Church in Tamerton Foliot, a slight frisson comes over me. The tree stands as a landmark for the area and the Copleston family history. Our heritage needs to be secured for future generations to learn from history and mistakes of the past.

❦ THE OLD TREE ❧

From antiquity, people have used distinctive trees for giving directions and Plymouth had a tree that did just that. It was known simply as the "Old Tree" or the "Great Tree" and is shown on some of the earliest maps and deeds. It is marked on Benjamin Donn's 1765 survey of Devon, which drew widespread acclaim for its accuracy, detail and draughtsmanship, so it must have been a tree of some stature even then.

The arboreal giant is long gone – thought to have been felled to make way for a new road – but almost a mile away there is a stone recessed into a wall on Greenbank Road near Mutley Plain on which can still be read: "The Way to the Old Tree, Kings Arms and Exeter Inn" on one face and on the other: "To the Old Town Gate 1754". The King's Arms was an important posting house in the early days of the postal service and stood close to the Old Tree on the main road out of town towards Exeter and London.

As well as the guide stone the tree's existence is recalled today by Old Tree Court, a tall office block built where there were four dwelling houses in 1837 next to Old Tree Slip between Lower Street and Exeter Street. In 1995 excavations in the area revealed the 17th century Old Tree Slip running parallel to Hawkers Lane. The mighty tree may have been gone for many years but its name lives on – the power of a tree.

Old Tree Court, Exeter Street.

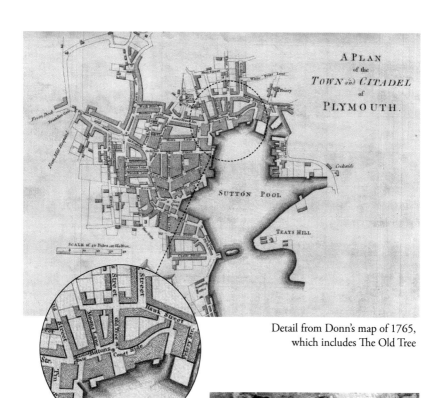

Detail from Donn's map of 1765,
which includes The Old Tree

Milestone marking the
way to the Old Tree.
Greenbank Hill, near Mutley Plain

❧ Bramley Bounty ❧

by Celia Steven

There have been many headlines about the Bramley and the King of Covent Garden certainly caught the imagination of the public in the early years when Henry Merryweather, my great grandfather, was explaining its origins to the media and public alike. At the age of seventeen he clearly recognised that this apple was something special and had great potential when he asked permission to take grafts.

But what is the story behind this famous apple and why is it called the Bramley? In the 1800s, a girl by the name of Mary Ann Brailsford who lived in Easthorpe, near Southwell, planted a pip from an apple in her garden. The pip grew into a tree which the family tended until they sold the house to Mr Bramley, who then took care of it. He must have given grafts to several people including Henry Merryweather. His only stipulation was that the apple should be called Bramley and so, the Bramley Seedling was born. The first recorded sale by Henry was on 31st October 1876. Over time it began to gather accolades and in 1883, at the Chiswick Fruit Festival it collected the much sought after Royal Horticultural Society Award of Merit, an achievement that underlined its importance.

The Bramley's value as a culinary apple grew and it was used extensively in both world wars to feed the troops and the population. As agriculture intensified in the second half of the 20th century many traditional orchards were grubbed up, something that caused me much distress as I knew how much wildlife was being destroyed. I had played in those orchards as a child; they were wonderful places to explore and enjoy, and seemingly always had a surfeit of apples to eat. Naturally there were Bramleys, one of the many varieties growing there, fruit that my mother used as part of our daily meals.

In 1973, when the UK joined the Common Market (later the EU), their grading regulations did not allow for a large sized cooking apple like the Bramley, because continental practice was to use second grade dessert apples for culinary purposes. I unwittingly mentioned this to a reporter at a friend's party and the next morning his wife arrived on my doorstep. Over a cup of coffee, she convinced me I had to do something about it. Quite a question, as I was a busy, young mother of two small children. However, I supposed it might be possible to send an apple pie to Mrs Godber, the wife of the Minister of Agriculture, with a letter containing a plea to the Minister to help the Bramley into Europe.

The delivery of such a pie with the help of my parents, created a lot of publicity, including taking part in a news broadcast at Pebble Mill, Birmingham with a tree in one hand and a basket of apples in the other. It was not long afterwards that the Minister made a public statement that the government would support the fruit industry and endeavour to get the apple categories changed to include the Bramley. When this was achieved later in the year, Joseph Godber attended a ceremony to plant a Bramley tree grown on its own roots from a cutting taken from the original tree. The Minister said he believed the Bramley was the best cooker in the world and he was confident that it had a great future on the Continent.

My part in the Bramley's history continued when I organised the Bramley Apple Pie Cooking Competition, with Council backing and the W I organising and training the judges. A great way to promote the Bramley and it worked. Over the years it evolved and has become the annual Bramley Apple Festival held every October in Southwell. It celebrates anything connected to apples and with all kinds of food and drink there, it helps to raise awareness about the importance of orchards and their contribution to biodiversity.

The years went by and the running of a horticultural nursery kept me busy. When my husband died the bank foreclosed on me and I had to leave. I left Nottinghamshire with a Bramley tree in the removal van, having just one weekend to find a home for my daughter and myself. We had lunch in Buckland Monachorum and decided that this village was a good place to live and we moved into our new home in 1998.

I was able to give the tree to St Andrew's School in the village and quite by chance that resulted in the setting up of a community orchard. This orchard has been a great way to educate children on the life of trees

Bramley Window, Southwell Minster
Reproduced by kind permission of Southwell Town Council

and nature surrounding them. So, my adventures with the Bramley apple continued. One particularly enjoyable activity was the result of the proceeds from the book, *Plymouth's Favourite Trees*, being spent in part on Bramley apple trees. They were enthusiastically planted in school grounds around Plymouth. I attended some of these events and it was such a pleasure seeing the different ways the schools treated their special day.

In 2009 there was great excitement as the Bramley reached its bicentenary and was celebrated all over the country. One of the highlights was a big service in Southwell Minster, attended by the great and the good, and incorporating the dedication of a Bramley window complete with the premiere of a new anthem commissioned especially for the event called The Tree of Life. I had never been to a service where the hymns, psalms and even the sermon were all about apples!

That year too, the Lord Mayor's Show in the City of London had a float highlighting the Bramley story which once again was an event to cherish. Down in the west country, the Princess Royal visited Cotehele, a National Trust property, where she planted a Bramley apple tree to celebrate this special year. Northern Ireland feted the great apple by holding a banquet, raising enough money to sink a well in Africa, which they aptly named the Bramley Well. Half of Britain's Bramley apples are grown commercially in Northern Ireland, the sixty original trees which started this venture came from H. Merryweather and Sons in Southwell.

There were so many other memorable occasions for me that year. Japan found me in Devon and I discovered there is a thriving Bramley Fan Club there. I have been to Japan twice since then – it was inspirational to see what they do with our famous apple.

Planting trees is of so much importance today, and apple trees enhance any area from a small garden to great orchards. As it says in the Bramley Apple book written by my brother, Roger Merryweather and myself some years ago, the Bramley is a world class, totally unique apple and makes an important contribution to the nation's diet with its versatility. As Henry Merryweather commented it is indeed, The King of All Apples!

❧ A WARTIME SURVIVOR ❧

There are many examples of trees which have withstood the devastation of war and one of the most remarkable in Plymouth must be the sycamore that stands next to the Guildhall in the city centre.

On the night of 21st March 1941 at the height of the Blitz in the Second World War, the Guildhall was set alight by incendiary bombs. The heat would have been intense as the wood panelling, floors, furniture and roof timbers caught fire. The following morning when this photograph was taken with fire hoses still primed, the building was nothing more than a burnt-out shell.

The heat must have scorched the sycamore, charring and cracking its fine-textured bark. Or perhaps a fireman doused it with water to keep it cool; who can tell? The evidence will be locked up in the pattern of the tree's annual growth rings but let us hope that it will be many more years before we have the opportunity to find out.

Sycamores are long-lived and their tall domed canopy makes an imposing sight. This one is the perfect companion to the Victorian Guildhall built in 1874 and it may have been planted at the same time.

Sycamore next to the Guildhall, 1941

Sycamore at the Guildhall, present day

After the war, a proposal to demolish the bomb-damaged Guildhall and replace it with a Beaux Arts design was rejected by one council vote in 1951. Today, the tree's presence works to unite the Gothic Revival style of the Guildhall with the strong character of modern buildings in the city centre.

MARKS IN BARKS
❧ OF LOVE AND LOSS ❧
BY HEATHER BARRIBALL

Screw your eyes up, stare beneath the superficial moss, ivy and recent scratchings, and you can just discern faint and distorted capital letters carved into the trunks of some mature trees as you stroll in Saltram Park. There are several scenic walks and cycle paths in the 500 acre parkland around the Saltram House National Trust property. It is hugely popular with Plymouth people enjoying exercise and bird watching.

Youths, lovers and passers-by have long indulged in the popular pastime of carving living tree graffiti, known as arborglyphs. In the case of Saltram Park, there are numerous examples dating from as far back as 1944. This is when American servicemen were billeted here to train and make preparations in readiness for the D-Day landings in France on 6th June 1944.

This ancient mixed woodland, dating from at least 1600, offered ideal concealment for the hutments and vehicles of the US 29th Infantry Division and other units passing through. Many of these troops departed on Route 23 along Normandy Way (previously named Vicarage Road) to Saltash Passage on the River Tamar for embarkation.

Surprisingly, many of these arborglyphs on the smoother bark of the mature beech trees are still visible. The young American soldiers, in a foreign land, might have been bored, lonely and fearful. They used their knives and bayonets to carve their initials, names, dates, designs (angel, star), and the names of home towns and states (Niagara Falls, NY, USA).

These historic WW2 arborglyphs are found on beeches scattered all over the estate, including Hardwick Woods to the north which was hived off by the A38. However, the most easily and safely spotted are in the wooded area along the tarmac track leading down from the main car park towards Saltram Point 'beach' on the River Plym. A fantastic example is inscribed on a magnificent mature beech which grows on the left a few minutes' walk beyond the cattle pens, opposite the next 5-bar gate. The large carving says Easter – perhaps this was the family name of a GI from Richmond, the capital of VA Virginia.

About 150 paces further along, off to the right, is a beech with very stretched arborglyphs of some names, initials and a star. Far over to the left is a younger beech with an arborglyph for Wisconsin 1944. Some 40 paces further along this wooded track and to the right, are arborglyphs which may be referring to Fall Brook Falls, Geneseo, which are an hour by road eastwards from Buffalo, the second largest city in New York State. Lastly along here, about 90 paces further down the track, on the back of almost the last tree on the right in this little wooded area, is another well preserved spectacular example of WW2 arborglyphs. One wonders who T. Miller was, carving his name so precisely, on the more sheltered side of the tree. USN usually signifies United States Navy.

There are many other WW2 arborglyphs along this stretch, and indeed all along the picturesque Riverside Walk. Most are now illegible, or spoiled by more recent carvings. However, much further along near the Saltmarsh is the Bird Hide. Just beyond it on the right is a mature beech, on which are carved the names EARL, HARRY, LOUISE and possibly, the place name MALTA MO – meaning perhaps Malta Bend in Missouri. Maybe it was a family back home, or a group of friends fondly remembered.

These living memorials are testament to the young soldiers who left their mark on history. Behind every initial, name and location, lies a story of love and loss.

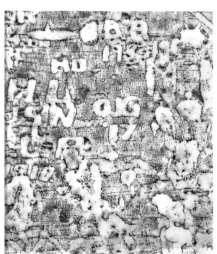 

Takuhon image and Heather and Judy creating a Takuhon imprint

❧ ELMS OF OLD ❧

When Plymouth Cricket Club moved to its new home at Peverell Park in 1924, the ground was noted for the fine elms around its boundary. For the next fifty years, they stood sentinel to the many games of cricket played there but disaster struck in 1971 with the arrival of Dutch Elm Disease and two years later, all twenty of the fully mature elm trees had been felled. It changed the way the ground looked and some would say how it felt.

The same sad story was playing out across Britain so it was no wonder that everywhere wanted new elms that would not succumb to the attentions of the bark beetle. In Plymouth's Central Park, half a mile from the cricket ground, an avenue of a hundred young elms was planted using the variety, 'Sapporo Autumn Gold', which came from a chance crossing between Japanese and Siberian elms. Following propagation in America, it rapidly became the 'gold standard' for disease resistance and was introduced to the UK in 1979.

Central Park's elms were planted soon afterwards. They have grown rapidly and make a lovely feature for all to see. Every summer, tree lovers have glanced anxiously into the trees' light green canopies to spot any brown patches, the first dreaded sign of Dutch Elm Disease. The avenue has stayed healthy although hedgerow elms nearby have suffered repeated cycles of infection.

Ode to Elm sculpture in Pound's Park

Elms seem to stir a particular passion in people and we read how elms were planted in the reign of George II as one of several measures to improve the appearance and amenities of old Plymouth. In 1736, plantings were recorded at Pennycomequick, Millbay and Frankfort

56

Elm Tree Avenue in Central Park

Gate. In 1752 the old Horse Pool outside Frankfort Gate was filled in and planted with sixty elm standards brought from Lopwell, seven miles away. Plantings in 1753 included "two rows from the top of Little Hoe Lane to the end of the walk on the Hoe" and the ground outside the Gate known as The Town Waste. An entry for 1756, however, which one hopes indicated official concern for the trees so carefully provided, states that "Tozer the Madman" cut down an elm tree!

Two hundred years later, the city authorities were similarly exercised by the need to plant trees and protect them from vandalism. A newspaper report from 1946 noted that young trees had been planted in many parts both before and during the war but "often in a matter of weeks they have been stripped of their foliage and branches and the small trunks adorned with grotesque carvings." The report goes on to state that it would be impossible to place guards around every new tree and all citizens had a responsibility to protect them, with their care and diligence being "amply repaid by the fine avenues that will appear and the thanks of another generation."

❧ GOING TO EXTREMES ☙

A stone's throw from the Widey Oak, in Widey Woods, is the Lucombe Oak. It is one of many Lucombe oaks, but because of its magnitude it is known locally as The Lucombe Oak.

Together with the Widey Oak this tree stood in the parkland grounds of Widey Court, the stately home where King Charles I was a visitor during the Civil War in the 17th century. The spreading crown of the Widey Oak and the more upright character of the Lucombe Oak can be seen towards the right of this engraving from the early 1800s.

The house was demolished in 1954 and new woodland has grown up around the ancient trees. There is a primary school built here today.

The Lucombe Oak is distinguished by its textured bark like that of a scaly reptile and its many branches which grow in spiralling patterns out of its massive trunk. The longest branch extends to nearly 18 metres. Buttresses around the tree's base are equally massive but a little tunnel runs between them through the tree's hollow centre. It is easy to imagine young rabbits playing hide and seek here.

Lucombe oaks are a hybrid between Turkey oak, *Quercus cerris,* and cork oak, *Quercus suber,* and were first raised in the UK by William Lucombe at his Exeter nursery in 1762. He liked his oak so much that

Widey Court

Lucombe Oak in Widey Woods

he felled the original tree in 1785 and kept the boards under his bed so his coffin could be made from them. By the time he died, aged 102, the planks had decayed and an alternative Lucombe oak, from one of his early graft propagations, was used instead.

❦ CHAPTER III ❧

HANDS ACROSS THE SEA

This chapter was going to be included as our contribution to the Mayflower 400 commemorations in 2020, but they were curtailed due to the Coronavirus pandemic. However, having received fascinating articles from both sides of the Atlantic, we felt that it would be remiss of us to omit them. Long may the friendship of our two countries continue and be sealed by the planting of trees.

Peaceful Canopies, Trees and Greenspaces of ❧ Plymouth, Michigan ❧

by Ellen Elliot

The city of Plymouth, Michigan, nestled between Detroit and Ann Arbor, is home to about 9,000 residents within its 2.2 square miles. For such a small footprint, Plymouth currently boasts 16 parks and recreation areas.

Having been chosen as a settlement in 1825, Plymouth soon became a thriving little town surrounded by wilderness and farmland. The importance of establishing and maintaining a village green was recognized by John Kellogg who donated land in the middle of the bustling town to be used as a restful gathering place for the inhabitants of the locale. Aptly named Park Kellogg this lovely green triangle has served the community well over the years. Heavily wooded at first, it eventually transitioned from a more formal memorial park displaying monuments from the Spanish-American and Civil Wars to a venue for summer concerts, picnics, and visits to the water fountain. It has also been a popular setting for weddings.

Many of the changes took place in 1968, and the *Plymouth Mail* reported "Beautification and conversion of Kellogg Park into a traditional 'village green,' replete with new pool, fountain, walkways and shade trees has been given an immediate go ahead by Plymouth city officials and considerable progress is expected to be made this autumn… Included in the plans will be gracious brick walkways, benches of wood and concrete for personal repose, plantings of new shrubs and the adding of new trees around the perimeter of the park. Relocation of 'Plymouth Rock' to another site within the park also is scheduled." Other monuments were also moved, including a cannon from the Spanish-American War which was transferred to the small park at the corner of Starkweather and Farmer Streets as well as the Civil War monument which was moved to Riverside Cemetery. These moves however would not be the last for the monuments.

In 2003, Plymouth experienced a tragic loss of a 150-year-old copper

Kellogg Park, 1906. Courtesy of the Plymouth Historical Museum

beech tree, *Fagus sylvatica* 'Purpurea', which was felled to make way for a housing development that never took shape and it provided a very painful lesson in tree preservation. Over time, as homes were demolished to clear space for new modern dwellings, trees were sacrificed in the process. This situation did not sit well with the residents of Plymouth. A tree ordinance was adopted in 2017 and revised in 2019 mandating the replanting of trees in proportion to those being removed. The concern over the loss of heritage trees was at the forefront, specifically trees with a diameter at breast height ranging from 8"-18" depending on the species. Over thirty different species were included on the list as heritage trees.

In response to the outcry over the loss of so many trees, a group of citizens, led by City Commissioner Kelly O'Donnell, rallied together in 2017 to form "Keep Plymouth Leafy" – a non-profit organization committed to "positively enhancing the leafy, tree-lined character of our Plymouth, Michigan streets and parks." Their mission to "grow and maintain a robust urban tree canopy in Plymouth, to provide important physical, aesthetic, recreational, and economic assets to existing and future residents of our city" is a driving force behind the reawakening of a leafy vision for Plymouth. Working with the Municipal Services department they have developed an impressive tree planting campaign centered on improving charm and desirability through the planting of trees and doing it in a way that is affordable for property owners. Conscious of the importance of species compatibility to the surrounds, the following trees have been chosen: tulip tree, linden, oak, sweet gum, London plane tree, and horse chestnut. Over 170 trees have been planted in the span of three years. The group has also given away 90 evergreen saplings for residents to plant in their own yards and hosted Arbor Day celebrations in the neighborhood parks, serving to bring awareness and education for the community on the importance of trees to the health and wellbeing of the environment and the beings who inhabit it.

Kellogg Park. Courtesy of Pete Mundt, 2020

Tonquish Creek, Plymouth, Michigan. Courtesy of Pete Mundt, 2020

The organization outlined ten reasons why Plymouth needs its trees:

Trees provide beauty.
They provide habitat for wildlife such as birds.
Trees clean our air, which leads to better public health.
Trees are natural windbreaks, which reduce heating costs in the winter.
Trees have sentimental value.
The color green is calming.
Trees reduce noise pollution.
Trees reveal the beauty in the changes of the season.
Trees increase home values.
Trees provide shade and reduce air conditioning costs.

The importance of maintaining a healthy tree canopy and unencumbered greenspace in the city of Plymouth has become a high priority for both city administration and the residents and will continue to honor the vision brought to light by John Kellogg so many years ago.

A Gift from Plymouth,
⸙ Michigan ⸙

Between the Civic Centre and the Guildhall in Plymouth, UK, there are Imperial Locust trees (also known as false acacias), which were given to the city by the people of Plymouth, Michigan in the USA. They were presented to the Lord Mayor, Alderman Frank Chapman, in July 1967 when he led a civic delegation to attend centennial celebrations of its incorporation as a township. Locust trees were planted as part of their celebrations too.

In exchange for the trees, a piece of granite from the Barbican was presented to the people of Plymouth, Michigan, which was later to be incorporated into the foundations of their new civic building. The granite was set on a plinth of black marble and flanked by bronze panels and became the centrepiece of a small monument comparable to our own Mayflower Steps.

The trees were planted in the Civic Square on 6th November 1967 during a tea interval of the monthly council meeting by The Lord Mayor, accompanied by Alderman H M Pattinson, Alderman Ron King and the Town Clerk, Mr Stuart Lloyd Jones.

Imperial Locust tree with The Guildhall, Civic Square

Planting in Civic Square, Plymouth in 1967

Together with the trees is a plaque, set in the ground, with the following inscription:

'IMPERIAL LOCUST TREES - THESE TREES, GIVEN TO THE PEOPLE OF PLYMOUTH, ENGLAND, BY THE PEOPLE OF PLYMOUTH, MICHIGAN, U.S.A, WERE PRESENTED TO THE LORD MAYOR FRANK CHAPMAN ON JULY 7, 1967, ON THE OCCASION OF HIS VISIT TO PLYMOUTH, MICHIGAN, U.S.A. WE OFFER THESE FOUR TREES AS A SYMBOL OF OUR RELATIONSHIP AND FRIENDSHIP WHICH WE FERVENTLY HOPE WILL CONTINUE INTO THE LIVES OF OUR FUTURE GENERATIONS. WE WOULD HOPE THE QUIET INFLUENCE OF THESE TREES IN OUR DAILY LIVES WOULD CAUSE YOUR PEOPLE TO EXPECT OUR PEOPLE TO REPLACE THEM AT THE END OF A LONG LIFE AND THAT OUR PEOPLE WOULD CONSIDER IT AN HONOR AND OBLIGATION TO DO SO'.

For several years after they were planted, an annual report by the Lord Mayor was sent to Plymouth, Michigan to be read at their Independence Day celebrations on the 4th July. It gave details about the condition of the trees and ensured the close links between the communities were maintained. A party from Plymouth, Michigan came to our city in 1970 for the 350th anniversary of the sailing of the Mayflower.

For the 400th anniversary in 2020 the Civic Square Locust trees were included in an American tree trail through the city centre. This walk is one of several and can be found on the Plymouth Trails app.

BREWSTER GARDENS,
❧ PLYMOUTH, MA ❧
BY ZACHARY LAMOTHE & SHELLEY KELLEY SULLIVAN

Three hundred years after the Pilgrim Fathers landed in Plymouth, Massachusetts a group of dedicated, imaginative women from the Plymouth Womens Club created Brewster Gardens. The site had been lined with industry, with mills of all kinds harnessing the water of the Town Brook to power the factories. Brewster Gardens was one of many projects undertaken in 1920 to clean up the dilapidated area of Plymouth's waterfront.

Of all the public parks in Plymouth, the crown jewel is Brewster Gardens, an idyllic greenspace that encompasses the perfect combination of natural beauty and historical relevance, along with an array of flora. Its location was the home lot of Elder William Brewster, one of the first Separatists, commonly known to history as the Pilgrims. He was the senior elder and religious leader of the colony, and eventually became an adviser to Governor William Bradford.

The Town Brook's fresh water was a primary reason for the group choosing this location as their permanent settlement along with the abundance of herring and roofing thatch which grew along the edge of the water. The Wampanoag people taught them how to fish for the herring and how to use them as a fertilizer for their crops.

The entrance to Brewster Gardens is on Water Street, close to the historic and vibrant Plymouth waterfront. Directly across the street is the Pilgrim Memorial State Park, which contains the landmark Plymouth Rock. Inside the park, about a quarter of a mile along the Town Brook is the Jenney Grist Mill. This was a water powered corn grinding mill constructed in 1636 which John Jenney, a colonist, had been granted permission to run. After his death, his wife Sarah and son Samuel ran it until 1683. The present mill is a reproduction built in 1970 and operated by the world-class living history museum, Plimoth Patuxet.

Nearby are monuments to Plymouth's immigrants and a tribute to the first Pilgrim women. The Immigrant Memorial is a piece of modern

Brewster Gardens

art, a silver oblong shape with numerous faces protruding from it. It was designed by Barney Zeitz, made of stainless steel and dedicated in 2001 to celebrate the immigrants over the centuries who have made Plymouth Massachusetts the town it is today.

The other more famous statue is that of the Pilgrim Maiden which stands over a small lagoon at the north end of the park. This was cast in bronze by the Anglo-American sculptor Henry Hudson Kitson in 1924. The statue was erected in recognition of the bravery of English women who persevered in their new home of Plymouth. The figure is of a young unnamed woman who is dressed in the traditional clothing of the period. A fountain sprays up in the lagoon in front of her and behind her is a small grove of pine trees.

Brewster Gardens has an abundance of flowers and trees. The sweet scent of lilac bushes, close to the Immigrant Memorial, wafts over the park, and is followed by the cream flowers of the oakleaf hydrangea. Even in winter there is color as a pine tree in the shape of a hook is blanketed in a swirl of red and white lights, making it the largest candy cane in town. Daffodils and the cinnamon fern announce the arrival of spring followed by a vibrant display of rhododendrons in late May.

From June to August three sedge varieties thrive in the wetland area of the garden: fox, tussock and three square sedge, along with river bulrush. Sweet flag grass is found at the water's edge. At the peak of summer, cardinal flower with its vivacious red, enriches the landscape. Other plant life including soft rush grass, the leafy arrow arum plant, the lavender blooming pickerelweed and the pointed leaves of the arrowhead can all be found growing here. Wool grass resembles its namesake as in season looks ripe for the picking. The colors of the Joe Pye weed and swamp milk weed add a dash of pink while the blue vervain adds purple. As the summer season wanes, the flowering New England aster paints Brewster Gardens with its pale hues.

Many other varieties of shrubs and trees can be found at Brewster here too, including the sweet pepperbush, swamp azalea, and the impressive dogwood trees. The yellows of the spicebush, the shadbush and the buttonbush can be admired here too. The highbush blueberry and the arrow wood viburnum both teem with berries.

The most visited tree may be one just outside the park. It is the Hitoshi Abe Memorial Tree. This is a Japanese maple tree that was

"The Pilgrim Maiden" in Brewster Gardens

planted on 9th August 2004 to commemorate a new friendship. Since 1990, Plymouth's sister town has been Shichigahama, Japan, and this tree was planted in honor of its longtime Mayor, the Honorable Hitoshi Abe who was Mayor during the commencement of the relationship between the two towns.

Brewster Gardens is the perfect park to visit at any time of the year. From the running of the herring in the spring to holiday lights in the winter, from the beautiful flora and the history steeped within its grounds it is exquisitely picturesque and is a must on most visitor itineraries.

❧ The Weymouth Pine ❧

When Captain George Weymouth anchored his ship, the Archangell, off the coast of Maine on 17th May 1605, it was with a view to exploring a land known to be abundant in nature. The expedition's recorder described it as "woody, growen with Firre, Birch, Oke and Beech, as farre as we saw along the shore..." The voyage had been sponsored by two wealthy patrons, Thomas Arundell and Henry Wriothesley with eventual colonisation in mind.

About five weeks later, on 16th June, Weymouth set sail for the return voyage to England with five captured native people on board. He had first won the trust of the local tribe, the Wabanaki, and then destroyed it by this inhuman act. He also brought back to England seeds of the eastern white pine, *Pinus strobus,* or the Firre tree that dominated the land.

In Maine today, fragments of the ancient forest remain in only a few places and, here, eastern white pine trees as tall as 75 metres grow happily in the close company of other trees, just as they did in 1605. Elsewhere, they and the other forest trees were felled for shipbuilding, industry and houses. The tall straight trunks of the eastern white pine were ideal for the masts of sailing ships.

Needles and cones of Weymouth pine

At first sight, it might appear that the tree was re-named the 'Weymouth pine' for the sea captain who discovered it and introduced it to Europe although his name is spelt in some records as 'Waymouth'. Another explanation is that a hundred years'

Weymouth pines in Central Park

later in the early 1700s, Lord Weymouth was a great advocate for the species and he planted many on his expansive estate at Longleat.

The needles of the Weymouth pine are grouped in fives and are soft and silky to touch. From a distance, the tree can be recognised by its straight stem surrounded by flattened sprays of needles which give it an almost fluffy appearance.

It was the enthusiasm for planting the pine as a valuable timber tree which encouraged the spread of the white pine blister rust, a fatal disease from Asia. It attacks five-needled pine trees and shrubs of the currant family like blackcurrants and gooseberries. Certain places in America will not allow currants to be planted in order to preserve their stately pines.

The blister rust thrives in warm, damp conditions so it is with some trepidation that we include the two mature Weymouth pines that stand in Plymouth's Central Park near Pounds House. Specimens of this size are not often seen and they deserve to be admired while reflecting on the tumultuous history that the tree represents.

❦ A Friendship Forged ❧
by Barbie Thompson

Millbay Park has a lengthy and intriguing past. A map from 1718 shows Mill Prison situated here on a tidal headland once occupied by windmills. Its position so close to the sea was considered not only healthier, but more convenient for the landing of prisoners.

Today, there are few reminders left with some lumps and bumps in the grass outlining buildings long gone, occasional flights of stairs leading nowhere; odd blocks of stone jutting through the surface, and, nestling amongst the grass are isolated patches of cobblestones. Edwardian gateposts frame the entrance into Millbay Park which was opened for public use in 1911 and is home today to a serene collection of mature trees.

The American War of Independence ensured Old Mill Prison was fully occupied. The buildings were reopened in May 1777 to take the overflow from hulks on the River Tamar. Two hundred years later, in 1997, the National Society of the Sons of the American Revolution

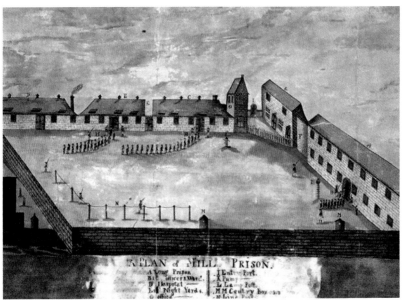

Mill Prison

74

Millbay Park

placed a plaque on the gatepost in Citadel Road. Upwards of 1500 men, mainly sailors had been incarcerated here.

Many Americans kept journals and they make interesting reading. Two main sources are New Englanders, Andrew Sherburne and Charles Herbert.

Sherburne gives a detailed description of the prison yard and buildings (the Americans were kept separately from the French). There was a gate leading into a courtyard where the cookhouse was situated. Fourteen-foot stone walls, topped with broken glass to the south and east, enclosed the area of approximately half an acre. The main gate was heavily reinforced with metal, and the inner gate sturdily constructed from wood. Herbert's journal reflects daily prison life and surroundings. His craftwork, which he sold at the Sunday markets, earned him enough to purchase extra food and luxuries, such as books which he loaned to other prisoners. He also taught himself navigation.

Many prisoners made special articles to sell, like coffee stalls, wooden spoons, punch ladles and bone ornaments, like those of John Deadman of Salem, who spent 22 months carving a rigged three-decker ship model, which he sold for twenty guineas.

News of the British surrender reached the inmates at Mill Prison via a London newspaper wrapped around a loaf of bread. The American prisoners celebrated by making a 13-Star flag from scraps of material thought to have been supplied by sympathetic locals. The flag remained with a Devon family at Chudleigh Knighton until the 1960s when it was sold at a Sotheby auction in New York for a figure containing six zeros to Claude Harkins, a member of US Sons of the Revolution and collector of Americana. It was tested by independent textile experts for authenticity and proved to be a genuine item made in the late 18th century.

June 1812 saw the start of the second and final conflict between Great Britain and the United States of America. Captain William Henry Allen was Master Commandant of the brig, USS Argus. On 14th August 1813, they encountered HMS Pelican off St. David's Head. During the engagement Captain Allen's left knee was shattered by a cannon ball. He surrendered his vessel after a short but fierce battle and Pelican sailed the captured Argus to Plymouth. The American surgeon on board amputated Allen's leg through the middle of his thigh. Landing

Door of Unity Annual Service of Remembrance on 16th June, Prysten House, 2016

Silver Maple, churchyard at St. Andrew's Church

at Plymouth, Captain Allen was taken to the hospital at Millbay Prison, where he died on 18th August 1813. He was buried with full military honours in St. Andrew's old churchyard. 500 marines and the Royal Marine band preceded the cortège. Captain Allen was laid to rest on the right of Richard Delphey, an 18 year old midshipman, who had lost both legs in the same action.

In 1930 a permanent memorial was installed in the old churchyard by the American organisation, 'Daughters of 1812'. It is set into the wall of the Prysten House next to the Door of Unity and its inscription gives thanks for the 'humane and chivalrous action of the English people'.

Nearby in the churchyard, there is a tree bearing the plaque 'Hands across the Sea'. It is a silver maple, *Acer saccharinum*, a popular tree across America and it commemorates the visit of the Plymouth Michigan delegation during the Mayflower anniversary in 1970. The inscription reads:

'LET THIS TREE FOREVER BE A SYMBOL OF THE FRIENDSHIP BETWEEN THE TWO CITIES.'

❧ Chapter IV ❧

Our Trees

Trees are so important to people's lives that occasionally they will go to great lengths to keep their special places leafy and well-tended. To achieve this often involves campaigning and fundraising as well as the more joyful activities of planting and caring for the young trees. At other times people wish to celebrate a national occasion or teachers encourage their pupils to take part in planting trees in their school grounds. Ownership of these great living things is important to people, hence the name of this chapter. So many of the glorious trees in our towns and cities are there for us and future generations to enjoy simply because of such efforts.

❧ CHERRY AID ❧

BY LIZ & ROY HARRIS

Living on a beautiful tree lined street, you would naturally wish to see this impressive sight continue. As residents of Torr Lane, we were happy to rise to the challenge.

Torr Lane is a busy through-road with 1930s suburban houses on both sides. It is thought that the narrow grass verges were not planted with trees until about twenty years after the houses were built.

The trees are ornamental cherry trees and came at a time of national popularity for their cheerful blossoms every spring. Similar trees, originating from Japan, were planted all over the country thanks to the endeavours of one man, 'Cherry' Ingram. His story is told in Naoko Abe's book of the same name.

The variety on Torr Lane is 'Tai haku' which translates as the 'Great White Cherry' so named for the colour and size of its flowers. They make a remarkable sight when all of the forty three trees are in blossom for just two short weeks at the beginning of April. It is one of nature's most eye-catching sights.

The lifespan of an ornamental cherry tree is relatively short at about seventy years, so it should have been no surprise when those in Torr Lane started to look time-worn. First it was leafless twigs and torn-out branches. Then 'surgery' was needed to make the failing trees safe and finally a stump was left. By 2013, there were eight gaps where trees once stood.

By good fortune, these losses coincided with a national tree planting programme called the 'Big Tree Plant'. It meant that the charity, Plymouth Tree Partnership, could provide eight replacement trees, whilst a team from Plymouth City Council could do the planting. They invited residents to participate and we spent a glorious rainy day digging holes and settling in our new trees, which had been growing in the nursery for seven years.

We were warned that this was the easy part and it would take several years of nurturing to get the trees established and growing well. My husband and I enrolled as volunteer Tree Wardens and learnt how to water the trees in summer, adjust the stakes and ties and prune to

Cherry blossom, Torr Lane

give them a strong and pleasing profile. It can be hard work to keep eight trees moist during a dry summer but Torr Lane is a friendly road and everyone took turns to come out with buckets and watering cans. We try to use rainwater from garden butts as much as possible. It is better for the trees and better for our water bills! As a reward the trees blossomed in their first year.

More trees were being lost to old age and by 2016 another nine replacements were needed. By then, there was no grant money available, so with our neighbours a few of us formed a fundraising committee. We delivered a letter to each house asking for donations. This time, we had to cover the cost of the new trees and labour to plant them, because the new sites had underground services running quite close, which meant a specialist contractor had to be employed.

There was a long and difficult discussion with the Council before they would give permission for the replacement trees to be planted. It seems that in an ideal world, roads would be designed so that service runs are in self-contained conduits and trees planted in forest-like conditions. In practice, however, modern infrastructure has developed in a random way, so tree roots and services have to share the same underground space. Without such a pragmatic acceptance, there would indeed be very few tree-lined streets that bring so much joy to our lives.

Torr Lane

The fund raising was boosted by the ward councillors making contributions from their community fund enabling us to reach our target. It meant that the planting could go ahead on a chilly winter's day. We kept the planting team fuelled with hot drinks and when the work was complete, everyone who had played a part came together for a celebration tea in the local church.

We planted another eight trees in 2018. Looking ahead, we can expect to replace more declining trees. Eighteen older trees remain, six of which are of differing species planted over the years. We do not know how much we will have to do ourselves or whether all the encouraging talk about the importance of trees will make a practical difference for streets like ours. Whatever happens, we are determined that Torr Lane will always have its trees.

❧ Our Beech Tree ❧
by Judy Harington

Mature trees lined Whiteford Road when our elderly neighbour moved here over 60 years ago, and many are now quite large. They span the road and reach out to the walls and rooftops of the three-storey Victorian terraced houses. They include horse chestnuts, Norway maples, limes and beech trees. They are sentinels, constant and reliable, welcoming visitors to the calm and security of the street, marking the seasons with their ever changing displays. They create a welcome distraction from the busy pace of modern life, enticing us to slow down and contemplate their serenity.

London has many streets like this, but such complete tree cover makes our street just one of a few in Plymouth. It is why we like living here although it does come with a price.

In spring, sticky pollen creates a gluey mess on parked cars. Catkins, seeds and leaves carpet the ground for much of the year, and many of the huge trunks take up all the pavement space so we are used to walking in the relatively quiet road. However all these inconveniences are minor and more than compensated by the pleasure and inspiration provided by such magnificent trees.

The canopy over our front garden is provided by a glorious common beech, *Fagus sylvatica*, known as the queen of British trees with her huge domed crown. I see her as a grandmother, spreading her protecting arms across the house. We watch pigeons and squirrels scampering high above the ground from upstairs windows, and see the setting sun light up her branches. The bark is mainly smooth and grey, warm to the touch. In spring the little red buds burst with uplifting, dazzling green foliage, followed shortly by the unobtrusive little catkins and flowers. The beech nuts are formed in spiky green husks which turn brown before dropping to the ground. Squirrels love them, and nuts that escape their clutches take root in the rich humus. It sometimes seems that we have our own tree nursery, and it is always a pleasure offering the seedlings to other neighbourhoods.

Druids believed that beech trees were the custodians of ancient knowledge. It is easy to believe that they might enhance wisdom and

A view of the beech from an upstairs window

creativity. The bark, leaves, nuts and flowers are all reported to have medicinal properties, especially for skin ailments, and young leaves are said to have a lemony flavour. In 19th century England, beech-nut oil was used for cooking and as fuel for lamps, and in France the nuts are roasted to make a type of coffee.

You can imagine that managing trees of this size in a residential road is going to generate different opinions. Everyone can see the positive benefits of preserving this wonderful leafy avenue but not everyone is so sure about the difficulties that the large trees undoubtedly cause. Fortunately the Council's tree experts have been totally understanding about the divergence of views and they have looked hard for ways of keeping the healthy trees while meeting the wishes of the residents.

When the time came for the much awaited tree maintenance work, the team was very chatty, informative and receptive. Chain saws make me nervous, so I had to trust that the men wielding them were well qualified for the task and sympathetic to our vision. That turned out to be the case. Our beech tree received a crown reduction of 4 metres, but it was 30 metres tall so it seemed like a light trim!

The importance of trees for our wellbeing, the ecosystems they

Tree experts at work

generate and the future of the environment, are increasingly recognised. The trees on Whiteford Road were planted before the motor car and modern living and over a century later are needed more than ever before. Thank goodness people had the vision to plant them and to keep them safe over all these years.

Grandmother Beech Tree

A poem by Cerowyn Browne

Thank you Grandmother beech tree,
for this moment of quiet in the mayhem of life,
you hold me in your strong arms,
my back against your solid branch
filling me with a deep sense of calm.

Let me grow to be like you Grandmother beech tree,
with deep roots to keep me grounded
and arms reaching up towards the sun.
Let me drink in the sunlight
but also dance in the storm,
let me sway in the gentle breeze
then be covered in snow,
let me withstand the downpour,
we all need rain, not just sunshine, to grow.

Let me let go like you Grandmother beech tree,
let my tears fall like your leaves in the autumn,
let me accept each branch that must rot and die,
I will learn from each cold and barren winter,
learn how to survive.
For when spring comes I can rejoice in each new bud,
cherish the unfurling of each new leaf,
not a single one will last forever,
but that is what makes them beautiful beyond belief.

Thank you Grandmother beech tree.

❧ SCHOOL TREES ❧

In 2008 the editors of this book had a great time compiling our first publication called *Plymouth's Favourite Trees*. We were fortunate to receive lottery funding to cover the cost of the book so all the sale proceeds could be used on planting trees. We decided that it would be good to have a project which involved schoolchildren in their school grounds; a great way to encourage the younger generation to enjoy the beauty of trees while cultivating a sense of ownership and a duty of care for the trees which they planted.

Invitations were sent to schools to ask if they could make use of our project. We were soon meeting headteachers and discussing the possibilities of where to plant, what to plant and who to plant with. All the staff were really supportive and we planted a vast selection of trees in over thirty schools. It was a most rewarding experience for us and we can only hope that the pupils benefitted as much.

It was an eye-opener at first to find that some children had never put their hands into as much as a window box, never mind dug in the garden. The simple joys of growing mustard and cress in a tray, or beans in a pot or even their own little corner of a garden had passed them by. It might lead to eager questions about what soil is. In answering we talk about the importance of keeping soil healthy. We go looking for worms, hear a shrill and turn to see a boy at the back trying to put one down the shirt of a child in front!

Coming back to the hole we have dug for one of the saplings, we point out the young roots, the stem and branches. We discuss how it started life as a seed, how tall it might grow and how long it might live. There is a brief silence as the children absorb the fact that many trees around them are older than their grandparents. Tree Wardens can play such a great part in educating the children in this way in their areas.

We show how to plant the sapling, then hand out trowels or small spades and divide the class into groups. Each digs a hole and we watch and encourage as they plant their tree. Occasionally, we are surprised to be asked which way up it should go! We stress that its future will depend on the nurture it receives in its early years and that they can help by watering it in summer. The questions start to follow in quick

yew

Drawing by Mia

Sliver birch
tree

Drawing by Una

yewtree

Drawing by Eva

willow

Drawing by Lila

succession and we do our best to answer each. Yes, trees do make their own food; yes, we depend on them for our oxygen and much more besides, and, yes, we all need to plant more trees.

Some of our most memorable school visits have seen us planting fruiting trees and shrubs under The Tree Council's banner of 'Hedgerow Harvest'. Their project lead, Jon Stokes joined us for those occasions bringing with him big bundles of apple, plum, elderflower, raspberry and hazel whips so the whole school could take part. We took elderflower cordial and different flavoured jams with us and after the tree planting lesson, we served refreshments made from 'Hedgerow Harvest'. It made a brilliant way to finish and brought home our critical dependence on the natural world.

We returned to each school about a year later to hear how the children had cared for their trees. The excitement still showed in their young faces and we will never forget their genuine enthusiasm in being able to take part. It was an unusual project to be involved in and here's hoping the proceeds from this book will lead to another generation of tree planters.

❧ HAM WOODS ❧

BY DAVE CURNO

Ham Woods is a large Local Nature Reserve in the north west of Plymouth. It has a small area of ancient woodland connected to the historic Ham House and the remainder is young or mature woodland or lowland meadow. The woods were formed by farmland purchases around 1980 and have some interesting features.

The urban stream flowing from a spring at Manadon to Weston Mill village captures attention and who doesn't like to listen to the sound of flowing water? In places it trickles over stones but also has pools where if you are lucky you may spot the eels which come here to spawn. It is no longer used to power the old mill, however the remains of the leat that was used to divert water to the mill can still be seen.

Some of the old farm fields were planted with trees but a few areas were left to develop as wildflower meadows, and recently restored they display a wide range of meadow plants. Unlike most wildflower meadows, these have never received artificial fertiliser so maintain the variety of plants and insects that would have been the normal makeup of a hay meadow for many centuries past. A popular place for a summer picnic and to listen to the crickets.

Then we have our trees, around 5,000 were planted in the 1990s and these are now maturing nicely. An area has been turned over to coppice to encourage more ground flora and to break up the height uniformity of the planted trees. Other areas of the woods have trees that have been growing for around a hundred years, maybe this was land abandoned from cultivation after the first world war? The ancient woodland area has a number of indicator species including wood anemone, dog's mercury and bluebells. In spring you will see a progression from the extensive yellow carpet of lesser celandine, to the white wild garlic (what a smell on a still day!) and then to the carpets of English bluebells, whilst the meadow becomes pink with red campion and creamy white with cowslip. There are also many hedgerow trees that have grown for most of their life unencumbered by other trees and have wide extending branches that once used to provide shade for cattle. Now these trees have younger neighbours but still dominate

Ham Woods

their patch of sky. The oldest are around 350-400 years old so started their life in the country and now live in a city.

Many of the old trees have holes and cavities which attract insects and grubs. As the holes get bigger they are populated by bats, small birds, woodpeckers, pigeons and doves. You will see plants growing on the upper branches of older trees and, along with ivy, these provide more nooks and crannies for insects and nesting birds. Inevitably, older trees lose branches or die and deadwood provides an important habitat for a range of insects, mosses and fungi. We have the usual mix of native trees as well as some more exotic ones, including three Monterey pines, a dawn redwood and a Lawson cypress, along with a recently planted Californian redwood, which at only 4 metres tall has a lot of growing to do!

The Community Orchard, planted by the Friends Group between 2013 and 2016 has a range of traditional and local fruit trees, including different apple varieties, pears, plums, cherries, medlar and walnut. Hidden away on a south facing slope, the area was completely covered in bramble which was cleared to plant the trees. Orchards are an important habitat and historic records show that there were at least eight in our woodland. Each farmhouse had a small orchard and there are areas of plum, apple and a very large pear tree, all of which are the remnants of a much larger historic orchard.

It is easy to see why Ham Woods is well-loved and well-used by local people and visitors alike. The affection shines through the activities of the Friends of Ham Woods which has a very active and far-reaching Facebook following. Regular posts point out new items of interest and quickly isolate any potential problems, meaning that a real sense of community ownership has built as a result.

I hope this may encourage many more people to visit the woods. There are some great circular walks some longer than others. If coming for the first time, think about bringing a map with you! A good way of doing this is to take a photo of one of the information boards which are near the entrances, of which there are many.

No matter how many times you visit Ham Woods and whichever route you choose, you will not be disappointed. There is such a diverse collection of interesting trees, birds, insects and wildflowers so just take your time to enjoy the peace and quiet of the woodland and the plants and animals that live in Ham Woods.

Ham Woods

❦ Coronation Avenue ❧

In 1937, children from schools across Plymouth were brought to the city's Central Park to plant an avenue of 150 red horse chestnut trees, *Aesculus x carnea*. Named for the colour of its flowers, the tree is a hybrid between the common horse chestnut which comes from eastern Europe and red buckeye which comes from north America.

The avenue planting was to mark the Coronation of George VI as king and his wife, Elizabeth, as queen. Planning was done in a hurry as this Council resolution passed just three months before the Coronation on 12th May 1937 shows:

"With regard to the proposal which has been approved by the Council for the planting of trees in Central Park in connection with the Coronation Celebrations, the quotation (750 shillings - £37.50 - per 100 trees) of J Cheal & Sons be accepted. In view of the urgency, the order be given immediately."

Cheals of Crawley was a well-known nursery firm founded in the late 19th century by Joseph Cheal. They propagated the trees by grafting the hybrid scion onto a rootstock and the high graft line is an unusual

Avenue of red horse chestnut trees, Central Park, Plymouth

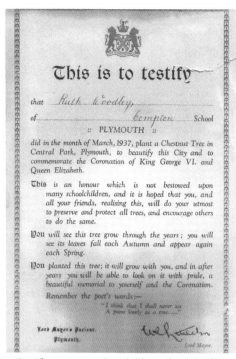

This is to testify

that _Ruth Woodley,_

of _Compton_ School

:: PLYMOUTH ::

did in the month of March, 1937, plant a Chestnut Tree in Central Park, Plymouth, to beautify this City and to commemorate the Coronation of King George VI. and Queen Elizabeth.

This is an honour which is not bestowed upon many schoolchildren, and it is hoped that you, and all your friends, realising this, will do your utmost to preserve and protect all trees, and encourage others to do the same.

You will see this tree grow through the years; you will see its leaves fall each Autumn and appear again each Spring.

You planted this tree; it will grow with you, and in after years you will be able to look on it with pride, a beautiful memorial to yourself and the Coronation.

Remember the poet's words:—

"I think that I shall never see
A poem lovely as a tree.—"

Lord Mayor's Parlour.
Plymouth.

Lord Mayor.

Certificate presented to children who helped with planting of Coronation Avenue

feature of the Coronation Avenue trees.

Ruth Heaton, née Woodley, was one of the children who took part and she remembered her day as a nine-year old like this:

"I was very excited about it and realised it was something very special. Four children – two boys and two girls were chosen to go because we were well behaved and had been good. We were pupils at Compton School situated in the heart of Lower Compton village at that time.

"We walked with an adult to Central Park. There were lots of other children there from various schools in Plymouth. There was a man there holding a young sapling which had been put into a hole in the earth. We took turns with a spade filling in the earth around the tree. It was all very exciting.

"For many years I tracked the growth of my tree as I called it. It was number thirteen on the right-hand side coming from the Barn Park Road entrance."

Each child who took part in the tree planting was presented with a certificate with beautifully chosen words. Ruth Heaton kept hers safe through the Second World War air raids on Plymouth and several house moves.

Seventy-five years later in 2012, Ruth and two other ladies from the Coronation planting, joined the Lord Mayor to plant the final tree in another new avenue to mark the Diamond Jubilee of Queen Elizabeth II.

❦ THE JUBILEE ROW PROJECT ❧
BY GLORIA

The whole idea began with a throw away comment at a Plymouth Tree Partnership steering group meeting in January 2012. 'Plant a Tree for Jubilee', was how it all came about! We thought something should be done to mark this momentous achievement and who better to organise it than the Plymouth Tree Partnership!

I heard myself volunteering to get the ball rolling as the first obstacle was lack of funds, so until we knew whether we could raise the money the project would never get off the ground. Armed with my briefcase I started by calling on companies big and small all over Plymouth. I only needed pledges for trees at this stage and by the end of 2 or 3 months, I had 68! Now we could really start to plan.

After meetings with Street Scene Services, we confirmed the plan of planting a new row of trees in Central Park to enhance Coronation Avenue planted in 1937.

During my visits to companies, I learnt that one of the children who had planted a 1937 tree was still alive, but unfortunately for us, lived in Australia. She had moved there on a £5 packet deal in the 1950s and although restricted to very little luggage, she took the certificate presented to her which she was given after planting the tree. This added another dimension to our project, there must be other people alive – a letter in the Herald revealed at least another 6 others, 3 of whom lived in Plymouth and were well enough to get involved with the new planting.

To show our appreciation to the generosity of the companies who had generously donated to our project, we had two display boards made, naming the avenue as Jubilee Row and listing the names of all the companies who supported us. These commemoration boards were erected at either end of Jubilee Row and have stayed there ever since.

The trees chosen were sweet chestnut, *Castanea sativa,* and *Zelkova serrata*. They line the path between the Clock Tower and Barn Park. Needing the help of children to do the planting, we invited students from Montpelier Primary, Plymouth College and Hyde Park Infants. Over 3 days, with the never ending support and help of Street

Some of the pupils from Plymouth schools who helped with planting

Scene Services, and what seemed like never ending rain, just like the newspaper had reported in 1937 when those trees were planted, over 350 children helped to plant in excess of 50 trees. Mrs Hassall, one of the veteran tree planters came to talk to some of the children, as well as Paris Cowan Hall and Jamie Lawrie, two players from Plymouth Argyle Football Club.

Many of our sponsors joined the Lord Mayor, Cllr Pauline Murphy, Cllr Tudor Evans, Leader of Plymouth City Council, Cllr Brian Vincent, Portfolio Holder for the Environment, at a reception held at the Tribute Lounge, Plymouth Argyle and afterwards the 3 lady veteran tree planters helped the Lord Mayor to plant a zelkova and unveil the commemorative panel by the Clock Tower. We sang the National Anthem and gave 3 hearty cheers for the Queen, before walking down the newly planted Jubilee Row.

It was a wonderful project. Clearly without raising about £10,000 from local companies and having the support of so many others to get the project off the ground, we would not have this lasting legacy for future generations to enjoy.

⸎ Chapter V ⸎

For the Love of Trees

Our appreciation of green spaces was never more apparent than during the lockdowns of 2020 when they were one of the few places we could visit. With time to 'stand and stare' we could wonder at the beauty around us, and at many times see and hear things never noticed before. Closer to nature, it got us asking questions like "How old is old?" and "How many things do trees give us?" Facts and figures are only part of the answer!

☙ Plymouth Pear Trees ☙

Three cities in the United Kingdom have trees named after them: London, Manchester and Plymouth. The London plane is ubiquitous and the Manchester poplar, a sub species of the native black poplar, was also widely distributed before 2000 when an airborne fungus, poplar scab, meant many thousands of the city's trees had to be felled.

By contrast, the Plymouth pear is one of the UK's rarest trees and protected by the Wildlife and Countryside Act. It grows discreetly in hedgerows and woodland margins in a few places in Devon and Cornwall, and only announces its presence when covered with sheets of pure white flowers. They make a remarkable sight in early May although their smell which attracts pollinating insects has been compared to wet carpets.

The Plymouth pear can easily be mistaken for a thorn tree which perhaps explains why its discovery came as late as 1865. It was made by the Victorian naturalist, Thomas Richard Archer Briggs, who was living near Eggbuckland at the time. His obituary noted his remarkable powers of critical observation, "at once so acute and so discriminating, his enthusiasm so real, and his industry so unflagging, that such a thing as a hasty, ill-considered judgment from him seemed always impossible. And

Plymouth pear in flower

his willingness to help was so unmistakable, that soon one learned to trust him whenever he declined to give a positive opinion."

The tree is rare because it produces few fertile seeds which seems to result from a lack of genetic diversity in the UK population as well as the cooler climate and it is more common in Western Europe, notably Brittany and Galicia. The circumstances of its arrival in Britain remain a mystery but it appears to be long established. It is thought that root suckers may have been brought here for use as hedging plants as the tree's lower branches have sharp thorns which make an impenetrable barrier.

There have been several recovery programmes that have involved controlled breeding, not using material from other parts of Europe in order to understand how the separate populations have developed. Grafted trees have also been grown by some nurseries although this is strongly discouraged because it perpetuates the lack of genetic diversity. Despite these initiatives the Plymouth pear looks set to remain an enigma.

❧ The Tale of the Church Pew ❧
by Eric Anning

About six hundred years ago I did not exist. The church buildings where my ancestors found their home existed but people generally stood or knelt to listen to readings and prayers. Sometimes there were benches around the walls for the old or infirm folk. Gradually we evolved from simple benches to quite grand and elaborate pieces of furniture that were moved around the building until our position at the centre of the space was eventually established.

From about 1500 we were generally owned by individual people who chose where they wanted us. Our church homes were often built by wealthy lords of the manor on their own property for the benefit of their family and tenants. Naturally enough these boss men wanted to show their status and so their artisans carved intricate designs on some of us. We were fixed to the floor and a few of us even had boxes built around to keep the draughts away from the people who sat on us.

From the Reformation in 1517 the length of church services increased; people wanted to be more comfortable and so we became more popular. When the people called Puritans started to preach really long sermons we were very much in demand.

By the Victorian era we had become firmly entrenched; it was almost as if we had always been a required feature of a church. We became loved and treasured by those people who sat on us regularly and were admired for our variety and beauty by the more casual visitor. It was a golden era for us. However, in 1844 a barrister called J C Fowler wrote in a paper about church pews -

"…pews are the cause of many quarrels and misunderstandings in parishes, almost all of which are attributable to the exclusive appropriation of them, any interference with which is looked upon as a trespass and invasion of rights, the danger and evils of which would be nearly extinguished by furnishing churches in a different manner."

This was alarming news for pews throughout the land!

As time moved on we discovered that some churches were being refurnished "in a different manner" so by the start of the third millennium we were often being replaced by chairs. Some of us have been taken into people's homes and are lovingly sat on over breakfast or put in the garden to better enjoy the sunshine. Others, God rest their souls, have been unceremoniously taken to the tip and made into wood pulp. But just a few of us have been able to take advantage of the versatility of the material we are made from - wood - and been recycled as tables, lecterns or other furniture in the churches we served. In that way we link the past, present and future so still have a purpose.

As a humble pew here is my story with a little support from a friendly kneeler and the help of a local woodworker.

Stoke Damerel Church in Plymouth was being refurbished and part of it involved my fellow pews being removed and replaced by chairs. The church needed a new Rectors name board because the old one had no space for additional names and as there was a good supply of oak pew wood the new board was made using some of that historic church timber. In addition there was a redundant kneeler that included carvings attributed to Violet Pinwill, an

An example of Violet Pinwill's work

accomplished woodcarver who, unusually for a woman in the early 1900s, ran a local wood carving business with her sisters.

The first job was to gently dismantle me and kneeler parts taking care not to damage the unique Pinwill carvings. This is always an interesting process. I could sense a bit of detective work to establish how we had been made and then working out how to reverse the process while maximising the available timber for the new project. There were pegged mortice and tenon joints, dovetails, tongue and groove joints,

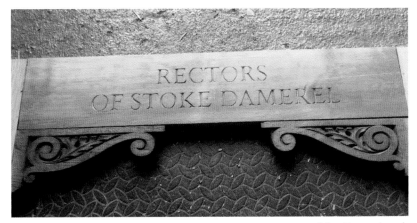

New Rectors board

screws hidden under wooden plugs and nails. Ouch! Most of our joints had also been glued. However over the 80-90 years since they were put together, most had dried out so it was not too painful when taking them apart.

Having dismantled the originals the timber selected for the new board was cut to size and planed. Over the years we and the kneeler had acquired a coating of stains, polish and dirt but having removed that the timber beneath the top surface was like new, but much better seasoned of course! Wood is such a lovely material to be made of, especially if your owner looks after it.

The two larger Pinwill carvings had been marked in pencil "Stoke rails", presumably by the carver, which was an interesting discovery. This has been preserved in the new Rectors Board although the writing can't be seen.

Our timber was machined to size and the joints made. Before assembly the legend "Rectors of Stoke Damerel" was hand carved on the top

Celtic style cross on the new board

106

piece of the frame.

To achieve the thickness of timber needed for the new board two outer frames were made and fastened together. This also formed the recess needed for the flat boards from our pew backs that would form the 'writing' surface. In assembling the board all the types of joint used in our and the kneeler's original construction were used as, although not necessary, it was a nice homage to the original makers, but I really wish the nails had been forgotten.

As the project was nearing completion the long uprights looked a little plain so two Celtic style crosses set into roundels were turned and carved by our helpful woodworker. The new carvings are quite simple so as not to detract from the more intricate Pinwill carvings. They also form a link between the top and bottom carved elements. This helps keep the craft alive and continues the tradition of ecclesiastical carvings.

When new we and kneeler had been stained to darken our wood. The original carvings incorporated into the new board were therefore a darker colour, in fact two different colours, to the planed timber. To remove the stain completely would have destroyed the carvings so the final job after sanding was to stain the planed timber to blend the colours.

So here I am repurposed as the new board and ready for Steve the signwriter to finish the job.

When I am finished I will of course go up in the world as I will be fixed on the wall! As I look out over those new chairs I wonder, what will the next 100 years bring?

Story as whispered to Eric Anning, woodworker,
while making the Rectors Board.

❧ Would you use Wood ❧

One of the beauties of building with wood is the way it results in human-scale structures, whether they be ships, buildings or bridges. Their size depends on what a tree can produce, not the rolling mill of a steelworks. It leads to many examples where wood has been used with great ingenuity in amazing structures that combine beauty and function. One thinks of the hammerbeam roofs of English Gothic architecture, or the way compass timbers were fitted to the sleek hulls of sailing ships or the elegant simplicity of a wooden arch bridge just as Monet painted it.

Wood has been used in the post-industrial world too and is still being used to make eye-catching structures. Brunel knew its capabilities and the railway he engineered between Plymouth and Truro shortly before his death in 1859 included 34 viaducts built partly or entirely from timber along its 70-mile length. Brunel used timber to keep construction costs down and, although he realised it would require more maintenance than masonry or iron, he anticipated this by choosing strong, straight pine logs from America and having them kyanised, often overseeing the process himself. Kyanising was patented by John Kyan in 1832 as a method for preserving timber against rot, and it involved soaking timber sections in tanks of bichloride of mercury mixed with water.

Brunel would not have known that the chemicals used in kyanising would corrode the iron fastenings used in the viaducts. However, he had designed them in such a way as to allow for easy replacement of any defective parts. Special gangs of men worked together on viaduct maintenance, reaching below the deck suspended from manilla ropes. The work could be completed without closing the line although trains were limited to 10 miles an hour until the replacement parts were properly in place.

Wood can be made stronger and less prone to warping without losing its aesthetic qualities by laminating, or gluing strips or boards together. The practice has been used since ancient times although plywood started to be produced on an industrial scale in the late 19th century and quickly found a diversity of uses.

Glulam, short for glue-laminated timber, works in a similar way but

A kyanised railway viaduct in Cornwall

uses layers of wood – often harvested from smaller trees – to form large structural beams and columns. It has a better strength to weight ratio than steel, looks far more attractive, requires less energy to manufacture and has much better insulating qualities. Furthermore, each glulam structure represents a long-term store of atmospheric carbon dioxide, locked up by the wood while living. These environmental benefits are especially important when designing for today's climate emergency.

Plymouth Life Centre, Central Park

Civil engineers and architects are becoming more ambitious with glulam uses. There are examples of road bridges that can take two lanes of heavy traffic, and buildings as tall as 18 storeys. Glulam pillars support the entrance to Plymouth Life Centre.

⁓ How old is old? ⁓

Trees are the oldest living things on earth. In a remote area of California's Sierra Nevada mountains, a lonely bristlecone pine nicknamed Methuselah is known to be nearly 5,000 years old. Its age was measured by core sampling in 1957 when it was over 4,789 years old.

In Britain, the oldest yews are believed to have been planted between 2,000 and 3,000 years ago, and they are mostly found on ancient sacred sites. It has been said that most trees are not as old as they look but yews are always older than they look.

In Plymouth the oldest tree is likely to be one of the gnarled oaks that escaped the shipbuilder's axe. They could easily be 500 years old and probably more. The adage goes that great oaks take 300 years to grow, 300 years to rest, and 300 years to die.

When discussing tree age, people usually think of the trunk and branches but sometimes the oldest part is the root system. Historically, people wanted poles much more than large trunks which were difficult to saw, and small timbers could be produced by coppicing. This involved cutting down trees to ground level so new shoots could emerge and grow to a useful size. The process was repeated again and again with coppice stools growing slightly wider with each successive cut over the centuries. The coppicing cycle means that the new shoots are always full of youthful vigour and the trees become almost immortal.

So far, we have only been thinking about individual trees but there are some species which can trace their origins to the era of the dinosaurs over 60 million years ago when ferns and conifers grew abundantly in the warm climate. The most famous is the dawn redwood, *Metasequoia glyptostroboides*. A Japanese paleobotanist identified its fossil in 1941 as a new genus, although one which was thought to be long extinct. Then in 1943, Zhan Wang, a professor at China's National Central University, was shown a tree which seemed to be important to the local people. Wang collected several branches and some cones but wrongly identified it as a variety of water pine. Three years later in 1946, the university sent an expedition to collect more samples from the same tree and, this time, with the war ended and having access to the earlier

Oak Tree with fallen branch, by Sylvia Hofflund

Japanese research, they declared it a 'living fossil'. The story caught the world's imagination, and the dawn redwood now flourishes in countless cultivated settings, although it remains critically endangered in nature due to human encroachment.

Something similar occurred in 1994, when the Wollemi pine, *Wollemia nobilis,* was discovered in New South Wales by David Noble, a parks and wildlife officer who was bushwalking with friends. They had abseiled into a deep canyon when Noble noticed the unusual nature of a pine tree growing on a narrow ledge and took a small fallen branch home with him for identification. It needed a team of experienced botanists to confirm that the same tree existed in the fossil records and was presumed to be long extinct. They named the tree after the Wollemi National Park where it was discovered and the person who discovered it.

Perhaps the dainty birch or quivering aspen are the longest-established trees in Britain. Pollen samples tell us that these pioneer species were among the first to cross the land bridge from the continent when the ice sheets melted about 11,000 years ago and before rising sea levels made Britain an island. Perhaps another fifty species made similar journeys and they are known today as native trees. Many more species have been introduced subsequently although some of them, like the familiar Christmas tree or Norway spruce, *Picea abies,* were present here before glaciation made their survival impossible.

We tend to think of tree fossils as being pretty leaf patterns in rock or coal seams. Even prettier is natural amber which is the fossilised resin of extinct pine-like species from between 30 and 90 million years ago. Amber beads are used for ornamental objects and jewellery, and they sometimes contain insects or other small organisms which were caught and enveloped by the sticky resin before it solidified and later fossilised.

Sometimes whole trees can be turned to stone or petrified. One of the most remarkable towers above visitors at the Natural History Museum in London and is 330 million years old. It was discovered in 1873 about 56 metres below the surface in a sandstone quarry in Edinburgh. Originally it was thought to be an ancient conifer but has since been identified as a type of seed fern, *Pitys withamii*, which lived

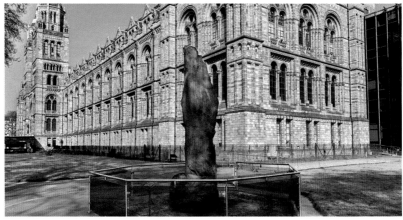

Fossilised tree, Natural History Museum, London.
Reproduced by kind permission of the Trustees of the Natural History Museum

112

during the carboniferous period. In the fossilisation process, the tree's organic matter was replaced by minerals with its weight increasing to three times that of normal wood and the tree keeping its original shape and structure.

So, just how old is an old tree?

❧ PAVEMENT PLANTINGS ❧

Without trees our city would be a sterile landscape of concrete, brick, steel and asphalt. Trees make neighbourhoods liveable for people by absorbing air pollution, modifying local climates, wind speeds, attenuating noise, and providing privacy and shade. People spend more time in tree-lined business areas, and well-grown trees increase residential property values by as much as 15%. They provide beauty to landscapes by their changes throughout the seasons, from their vibrant greens through to their autumn colours and even their bare branches. They have the ability to help people to relax, to relieve stress levels and provide a reason to visit whether it be a park, woodland or shopping centre. Without trees our world would be a far worse place. Trees provide some of the necessities of life; wood, food and oxygen as well as absorbing carbon, cooling our towns and cities, providing a home for wildlife and improving our health and wellbeing.

Trees are forest dwellers and coping with the fractured eco-systems of city streets is very stressful. So, how do we create the conditions for them to succeed on pavements where there are no carpets of nutrient-rich leaf mould and rainwater is channelled into drains? There are two main approaches depending on whether sites have had a tree growing previously or never been planted.

Most pavement trees were planted before the first world war and many have been lost to old age and decay; their former existence being marked by a stump or a sunken patch of tarmac. These trees and the remains of trees started their urban lives when the ground was relatively soft and underground obstacles were few. It gave them time to spread their roots beneath the pavements and into the rich soil of well-tended Victorian and Edwardian gardens. Since then, the growing environment has become more hostile with ground compacted by motor traffic, front gardens paved over, and pipes and cables everywhere. It would seem an impossibility to establish a replacement tree in such unpromising conditions, yet this is not the case. It works because the root runs of the original tree provide a network of nutrient-lined tunnels which the roots of the new trees can exploit. This natural framework makes one more unexpected gift bestowed by the original trees.

Where hard landscapes have never had trees, it becomes a real challenge to plant them. The problem is how to support a pavement so that it will bear the weight of pedestrians and motor traffic while providing enough uncompacted and watered soil for the new tree. It is only recently that practical solutions have become available and soil cells are starting to prove their worth. They are made from recycled plastic and look a little like old-fashioned milk crates. When installed in the tree pit, they rest on a solid base and are strong enough to provide the necessary support. All the spaces between the cell walls need to be filled with soil and connections made so water and air can reach the roots. There are many examples where soil cells have been fitted around existing utility runs and the system makes a permanent installation which does not need to be touched should a replacement tree become necessary.

Trees are increasingly regarded as part of mainstream urban infrastructure for all the benefits they bring. With this appreciation and with growing knowledge and experience, it is certain that many more of the old gaps will be replanted and many more places found for new trees on city streets.

Planting trees in Haddington Road

Branching Out
⚘ with Facts & Figures ⚘

What is a tree?

The dictionary definition of a tree is a woody perennial plant, typically having a single stem or trunk growing to a considerable height and bearing lateral branches at some distance from the ground.

The tallest

The coast redwoods, *Sequoia sempervirens,* of California are the world's tallest trees. One nicknamed Hyperion was measured in 2006, by climbing with a direct tape-drop, and found to be 115.55 metres which is nearly as tall as the towers of the Tamar suspension bridge. Hyperion is situated in the Redwood National Park but, even so, 96% of the original coast redwood growth has been logged.

The tallest that a tree can grow is thought to be 120 metres which is the maximum height that it can draw up water from the ground. The leaves at the top of a tall tree are always smaller than those at the bottom.

The largest

A hundred and fifty miles inland from the Californian coast is the mountain home of the giant redwoods, *Sequoiadendron giganteum,* in Sequoia National Park. The largest of these is nicknamed General Sherman which is reckoned to be the largest living thing by volume measuring 11 metres in diameter and 83 metres in height. Giant redwood is sometimes known as Wellingtonia in Britain as it was introduced here in 1853, the year after the Duke of Wellington died.

The largest tree in Plymouth is probably one of the Monterey pines, *Pinus radiata,* which can grow quite tall in the mild southwest but struggle to reach any height on their native cliffs of the Monterey peninsula in California. One in Central Park has been a favourite nesting site for ravens.

Inspiration for a lighthouse

Plymouth's famous land-mark, Smeaton's Tower, was inspired by the shape of oak trees. John Smeaton noted how their flared base and tapering pillar provid-ed strength and flexibility when buffeted by storms. His lighthouse, the third on the Eddystone Reef with-stood the fiercest storms for 123 years. It was dismantled in 1882 on account of waves eroding its underlying rock and rebuilt as a memorial to Smeaton on the Hoe.

Smeaton's Tower on Plymouth Hoe

Does it float?

Some tropical hardwoods are so dense that they sink in water. Ebony is one although the best known is Lignum vitae or ironwood. It is so named because hand tools cannot cut it and it has to be worked by machine. In the early days of steamships, Lignum vitae was used to line the underwater bearings of ships' propeller shafts. Today, the species is on the critically endangered list.

Defending themselves

Trees can sense when their tissues are disturbed by nibbling insects, browsing animals or even the forester's saw. This is because all aspects of their growth are regulated by hormones which are connected through the tree by long pathways. When these pathways are interrupted the tree goes into hormonal overdrive which stimulates the affected cells to produce protective chemicals or secretions such as resin. This means it is important to know how to prune properly which is something that tree professionals and volunteers with The Tree Council's Tree Warden scheme are taught.

❦ STAND AND STARE ❧

Every town has trees that do not seem to know the rules and it is their quirkiness that draws people to them. Here are some in Plymouth where you may find tree spotters stroking their bark or gazing up into their canopies.

The umbrella tree – Devonport Park

A small tree in Devonport Park hardly gets a notice in summer with so many fine trees all around but when other trees have lost their leaves in winter, it comes into its own. People head towards it for its glossy, apple-green foliage and spreading umbrella shape, and it is indeed useful for sheltering under in a shower.

The tree is a New Zealand Broadleaf or Kapuka in Maori, although more commonly known by its botanical name *Griselinia littoralis*. The genus is named after Franc Griselini, an 18th century Venetian botanist whilst 'littoralis' means 'by the coast'. Griselinia needs a mild climate to grow well and it is commonly planted as a seaside hedge.

Griselinia tree, Devonport Park

The Amur cork tree, King Street

The Amur Cork tree – King Street

Fastigiate trees, or those with narrow, upright canopies are often chosen for planting in towns and cities where space is limited. The Amur cork tree on King Street near Plymouth's city centre is the exact opposite. It is wider than it is tall and spreads expansively over the pavement to caress the sides of passing vans and lorries.

Amur cork trees originate from north-east Asia. Their bark is a smooth yellow grey when young, becoming thick and corky with deep furrows at maturity. The Chinese use the bark as a traditional herbal medicine and it is used more widely as a health supplement.

The tree's glossy green compound leaves turn yellow in autumn and fall early in the season to reveal a twiggy, flat-topped profile. It is an unusual tree but a useful one too.

The maidenhair tree – Thorn Park

Close to the south-east corner of Thorn Park in Plymouth is one of the country's largest maidenhair trees, *Ginkgo biloba*, with a girth of 3.2 metres. It is easily recognised by its branches that stretch upwards like a hand trying to grasp a fruit that is just out of reach. Its trunk is starting to show the characteristic swellings seen on ancient Chinese trees whilst its deciduous leaves are like those of a maidenhair fern, not having a central vein. Ginkgo's flowers are either male or female and borne on separate trees. Male clones are usually chosen because the brown date-like fruits of female trees are supposed to have a strong putrid smell. However, the Thorn Park tree is female and its fruits have not been a problem so far. Perhaps the best time to admire the maidenhair tree is in autumn when its leaves turn a rich buttercream colour and make a vivid contrast to the russets and golds of other trees.

Leaves of maidenhair tree

The giant's bench – Saltram House

This amazing sycamore, *Acer pseudoplatanus*, stands in the middle of the National Trust's car park at Saltram House. Its linear, ground-hugging bole would make a good seat for people ten times taller than today's visitors. In fact, there would be several giant seats, each formed between the ascending sturdy trunks which grow sculpturally out of the bole. Opinions are divided about the tree's origin although most believe it started life as a hedgerow stem that was laid in a way which caused it to sprout new shoots and then roots. Another theory is that several saplings were planted together for a playful purpose, perhaps to make

'The Giant's Bench', Saltram Park

a lovers' bower or a peekaboo place for children. However it began, the tree or trees have fused together, and their buttresses and roots now form an unusual feature of remarkable natural beauty.

❧ FOOD AND FURNITURE ❧

Ask most people what foods come from trees and the chances are they will answer: apples, pears, cherries and plums. If they think a little longer, they might add: walnuts, chestnuts and hazel nuts. Some might also think of our warming climate and suggest apricots, olives and almonds.

Honey might be a connection too far unless they are standing beneath a lime tree in flower on a warm sunny day. The rhythmic droning of bees as they forage on the tree's sweet nectar is surprisingly loud. The nectar from each flowering tree species has a different flavour and honey connoisseurs can tell them apart.

Forest honey, however, does not come from flowers. It comes from bees foraging on honeydew, which is the sticky substance left by aphids and other insects as they chew on leaves. Forest honey is darker and more treacly than floral honeys, and it makes an excellent accompaniment to porridge.

Wherever you live, there will be wood all around you. It may be a door or windows, the floorboards or even the structure of your house itself. But the most obvious wood in your home will be the furniture. Even if we don't have any money we can scrounge some orange boxes and yes, they too are made from wood!

There are many different timbers used in furniture making with

perhaps the finest pieces coming from walnut or mahogany. More plentiful and widely appreciated are the warm honey tones of pine with its wavy grain and nut-brown knots. It is a cheerful wood for a child's bedroom or maybe a study. Teak also gives a golden hue, but unlike pine is hard, durable and knot free. It comes from the Far East although in furniture is sometimes known as Danish teak because their designers used it extensively in the 1950s and 1960s. The style is instantly recognisable for its elegant simplicity, and it is still seen at the heart of a family in kitchens and dining rooms.

Craftspeople are attracted to many other timbers, some of which come from parks, orchards or even streets, and not originally grown for furniture making.

The grain and colour variations in wood are the main reason for its attractiveness. Heartwood, the older, inner section of a tree, is usually darker than the surrounding sapwood which acts as a pipeline for water to travel up the tree to the leaves on all the branches. As a tree grows and expands in girth, sapwood cells progressively dry out and become heartwood, adding to the tree's strength at the same time. In some timbers the colour change between heartwood and sapwood is quite distinct whilst in others it is more subtle.

There is skill in deciding how to cut timber for the best effect in the finished article. Much depends on the grain pattern which is able to tell us both the identity of the tree, as well as a great deal about its life. In places with a seasonal climate outside the tropics, annual rings are formed as trees grow rapidly in spring, rather slower in summer and become dormant over winter. Spring growth or 'earlywood' is lighter than the darker, summer growth of 'latewood'. The resultant rings are more pronounced in some tree species than others whilst changing weather conditions are a big influence in every case.

The next time you are sitting at your table, stop to wonder exactly where the wood has come from and everything involved in bringing it to you. We have so much to thank nature for when she gave us the humble tree.

❧ Reflections ❧

Strangely it often seems that we like to see trees in straight lines, in rows and avenues. It is not how they grow in a forest and perhaps it gives us a sense of order in the concrete jungles of towns and cities with their conflicting building patterns, random traffic movements and discordant noises.

In parks and gardens too, tree avenues help us navigate through their more natural landscapes and in doing so provide a sense of journey.

In orchards, we find trees invariably planted in a grid pattern to help with management and harvesting. So it is with the neat, boxed rows of clipped citrus bushes in the orangeries of stately homes like Saltram House in Plymouth.

There is a tension between our desire for order and structure and for letting nature's giants express themselves in their own way. We want trees close to us for the benefits they bring but can we be accused of using them like green statues and treating their fruits as objects? The dichotomy is captured by this original poem which was given to us when producing the book and which seems a thoughtful way to end it.

Ha! Part of a still-life, says he,
An orange born in an orangery
Something to paint, sketch quickly down,
Watch how he wears a fauvist frown
Each stroke a masterstroke he claims
Yet with each one my body tames
And in his daubs of a living face
No thoughts of freedom find a place.
Would he but see a far-off grove
In a setting sun of fiery mauve
Then he would sense the poignancy
As dusk falls on the orangery.

The Orangery at Saltram House

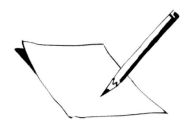

❧ THE AUTHORS & ARTISTS ☙

Little did we realise when we started out on this book that it would stir so many passions within our contributors. We just hope that it has inspired some of you to maybe plant trees or offer your services as a tree warden wherever you live. Whatever you do, whoever you are, we thank you most sincerely for your interest and hope the book has brought you joy. Read on to discover more about the people who made it possible.

Eric Anning

Looking back, my interest in wood as a material was kindled at school. In my days practically all secondary schools had woodworking or metalwork on the curriculum. My more specific interest in making turned objects started almost by chance in 1997. After enrolling in weekly evening classes on a course led by Tobias Kaye, a professional woodturner, my rewarding hobby was launched. In 1999, I met three or four other people sharing the same hobby and we decided to form the Plymouth Woodturners Club. I have been involved with the club ever since.

Chris Avent

I live in the beautiful Tamar Valley with my lovely family and enjoy spending as much time outdoors as possible. I love fruit trees and have a growing number of them in the garden surrounding the veg beds. Food growing and nature have been a passion which has been with me since growing up on a family run market garden on the edge of Plymouth. I believe we cannot grow as a society until we provide an economy, landscapes and lifestyles that recognise the true value of natural systems and our relationship with and responsibility towards them.

Heather Barriball

Over the years, my relationship with trees has been changing. At first, I regarded trees only as living objects in the landscape; branches to climb as a child, leaves in the gutters to curse as a householder, a resource to use for discovery and learning during my teaching career. More recently however, I've been realising the spring arrival of hazel catkins, blackthorn, mimosa and pink cherries herald not only a glimpse of warmer seasons, but also hold happy family memories. After doing some research for the American Tree Trail, I no longer take trees for granted. I realised my joy at uncovering the ways trees can be the repositories of our sentiments and activities. Tracing people's shared histories with trees has become a fascinating interest for me. To view the American Tree Trail, download the Plymouth Trails App free from the App store. Acknowledgement is made to Chantel Summerfield and staff at Saltram who did much of the original research of all types of arborglyphs across the site in 2010.

James Brown

I am a member of the Chartered Landscape Institute with a post graduate qualification in Urban Design. Having worked for the environmental charity Groundwork for thirteen years designing and delivering landscape improvement projects on behalf of communities and landowners, most recently as Principal Landscape Architect, currently working freelance, with a particular interest in nature and trees, their benefits to people and their contribution to place making. Inspired by the principles of Biophilia, I have written and presented papers on the Benefits of Nature for conferences in the South West including the University of West England Communities Research Forum.

Paul Copleston

I am 100% Plymothian. Born in a prefabricated house at West Park in 1963, I was educated at Knowle Primary School and Sutton High School for Boys. I enjoyed growing up in the 1970s with my brother Mark, and although living in what would now be called poverty, we both managed to find a way to break free and secure jobs and homes. Unknown to me at the time, the view in the distance, from the landing window of our council house, was partly of land once owned by the Coplestons, namely Warleigh House and its surrounding lands at Tamerton Foliot. Having retired in 2020, I have more time to follow my hobbies as a keen genealogist, photographer and Plymouth Argyle fan. Having discovered that the Copleston family could be traced back to at least 1200 in Devon, I have embarked on digitising records and created the web site: *www.copleston.net.*

Dave Curno

I live just a few hundred metres from Ham Woods and have been involved with the Friends Group from when it was first set up in 2013. I have an interest in trees, woodlands and woodworking, in particular green woodworking as a traditional way of making furniture. My leisure time is taken up with sailing, which is also an excellent way of looking at trees.

Sue Dann

I have decided trees grow on you over time. As I have got older I have realised nature has a real impact on my well-being. Trees represent life, we put down roots, we grow, we blossom and every year we get the opportunity to throw off all our leaves and start to grow again.

Oliver Dixon

My hobby as a photographer started when I was about ten and I could borrow my grandad's SLR camera. Several of those early shots include some unusual compositions which still give me a slight buzz when seeing them again. My interest in trees started at about the same time when my gran took me to tree plantings organised by the Plymouth Tree Partnership and I soon became a useful member of the team. As both these interests developed, I found myself able to capture the beauty of trees at their best and help others appreciate them. In my working life, I have recently completed my apprenticeship as an electrician and am looking forward to taking more responsibility for the complex systems we have to look after.

Editors' note: We owe our thanks to Oliver for patiently seeking out the trees we chose and finding the best times and places to photograph them.

Ellen Elliott

I am an historian and lecturer specializing in the history of Plymouth and Northville, Michigan. My interests include historic architectural preservation, vintage photography and genealogy. I am an assistant to the archivist at the Northville Historical Society and volunteer in the archives of the Plymouth Historical Museum. I am the executive director of the non-profit organization Friends of the Penn and manager of the historic Penn Theatre in Plymouth, Michigan. I also serve on the boards of the Friends of the Plymouth District Library and Plymouth Downtown Development Authority. I hold a Bachelor of Science degree in Chemistry from Madonna College.

David Frost

I have spent most of my working life in construction as a surveyor and estimator, but was always interested in the natural world. When I retired, I volunteered for the National Trust and the Devon Wildlife Trust. As a longtime supporter of the Woodland Trust I also assisted with the reviewing of planning applications, where there could be conflict with ancient woodlands, ancient and veteran trees. My ability to interpret drawings from my construction background helped. I also trained with the Woodland Trust as a verifier for their Ancient Tree Inventory database and have been a volunteer with Plymouth Tree Partnership for several years. Trees are all around us and I can always be seen looking skyward or hugging them!

Judy Harington

I am an Environmental Artist concerned with increasing awareness of our place in nature and the world, and what we can do to live more sustainably. After a successful career in the NHS, I took up a long-held passion for art and graduated with a BA in 2019. I work in many different media, including painting, printmaking and ceramics.
For more information contact Judy at: https:// judyharington.com

Editors' Note: We are grateful to Judy for producing the Takuhon prints. Takuhon (ink rubbing) is an ancient Japanese art of print making. The Japanese washi paper is dampened and pressed into the detail of the object and allowed almost to dry. Then ink is sparingly applied using a tampo or pad and pressed vertically into the object.

Liz & Roy Harris

For a fortnight each year the blossom of the cherry trees in Torr Lane is considered one of the most delightful sights in Plymouth, followed by the display of autumnal coloured leaves. We were certainly influenced in moving to the area thirty years ago by the presence of these trees lining both sides of the street. However, by 2013 several of the trees had died. This spurred us into action and after a huge amount of work with other residents, so far we have replaced 25 trees and we are now Tree Wardens for Torr Lane tending the young trees in readiness for future generations to enjoy.

Sylvia Hofflund

I earned my degree with Honours in Fine Art Painting and Illustration from the Art Center College of Design in Pasadena, California. Over the past thirty years I have created images for advertising, publishing, packaging and design firms. I moved to Plymouth, England in 2011 and continue to be inspired by the natural world.
Examples of my art work can be found at: sylviahofflund.com

Shelley Kelley Sullivan

I was born in Boston and am currently living in Plymouth, Massachusetts. It is no surprise that it has been discovered that trees communicate with each other. There is a distinct energy that is felt in their presence. As indigenous people around the world believe, every tree has a life, a spirit, a name, I too believe they are sacred. Trees are the great sentinels on this earth and keep a steadfast watch. Inspirational writer, Joanne Raptis, wrote a beautiful quote about trees offering wide advice for all of us to follow: "Be like a tree. Stay grounded. Connect with your roots. Turn over a new leaf. Bend before you break. Enjoy your unique natural beauty. Keep growing"

Zachary Lamothe

I am a writer based out of Plymouth, Massachusetts. Originally from Connecticut, I have written two books about the offbeat and odd in my home state. In Massachusetts I have penned the book A History Lover's Guide to the South Shore. Currently I am working on a restaurant guide linked to Boston. I am a frequent magazine writer and write the travel blog "Backyard Road Trips" (*www.backyardroadtrips.com*), which is also a podcast that I co-ordinate.

Ali North

I am a wildlife conservationist and PhD researcher currently based in Plymouth. As a keen rock climber and nature enthusiast my love of trees stemmed from a childhood (and subsequent adulthood) spent climbing them!
My website is: https://leafylocals.wixsite.com/leafylocals.

Chris Robinson

Interesting articles are published in the Herald weekly by one of the City's foremost local historians, Chris Robinson, who has also written over 40 books on different aspects of Plymouth and the surrounding area. Educated locally, he is a third generation Plymothian and a keen advocate of all the City has to offer.

Find out more at: www.chrisrobinson.co.uk

Jess Slocombe

When Gloria and Andrew approached me to produce the layout design of the book, I was immediately attracted to this commission. I was lucky enough to grow up in a village and, perhaps because of this, living in a city would seem bleak and barren without trees and the life they bring. The natural world is very important to me and I've always been particularly drawn to trees, which is part of the reason I was keen to be involved. Books can be especially rewarding to work on, from the outset Gloria and Andrew had a clear idea of how they wanted the book to take shape and I hope I have successfully realised this for them. They have been a pleasure to work for and a key element in making this an enjoyable project for me.

Editors' Note: We are grateful to Jess for her unfailing enthusiasm and patience in producing the book.

Celia Steven

Trees are a way of life and an inspiration. They are memories of youth and listening to the wind blow through the branches of a row of old elm trees I was particularly fond of when walking to the farm to collect milk, or to see a ghostly owl flying out from the orchard in front of home on a moonlit night. Growing and planting trees is something I do to this day and hope that it gives encouragement for other folk to do the same. I continue to learn more as the years pass, not to mention the growing value of the need for trees and why they are important. It doesn't matter what time of year it is, a tree is a delight, whether it be a silhouette in the winter, the joy of fresh leaves in the spring, the sounds surrounding the trees or the beautiful flowers and blossom that adorn them. I always think the countryside looks as if it is a wedding celebration, when the hawthorn comes into flower. The older I get the more I love trees, and they have always figured in my life in one way or another.

Barbie Thompson

I grew up in Plymouth and was educated at Plymouth Secondary School for Girls where I studied commercial subjects, leading to a career as a PA taking me to London, the Middle East, and North Africa. Returning to England in 2000, retirement has allowed me time to resume my childhood fascination with history. With the support of the Plymouth U3A Shared Learning Project, I have presented a series of papers relating to maritime history and the Napoleonic Wars. My love of trees stems from my love of history.

Kevin Tole

From a very young age I have always been able to lose myself in the magnificence of trees, woods and forests. I think it comes from an early sense of independence being the eldest in my family, the desire to climb a high tree or to lose yourself in a deep thicket. My career in art has taken me back to that deep abiding oneness with trees and this has been further pursued with my membership of the international art group, The Arborealists. Plymouth and its hinterland are well served with magnificent individual trees and magical woods. These have all inspired me a desire to share their magnificence through my art work. *My website address is: www.kevintole.com*

Jane Turner

I was born and raised in a village near Cardiff. I always loved being outdoors and did a lot of walking with my family. My first experience of volunteering was as a resident warden on Skomer Island, where I saw my first Manx Shearwater. After finishing a degree in Geographical Science I decided I wanted to work in Ecology/ Conservation, so volunteered with the British Trust Conservation Volunteers (BTCV) and eventually supervised the project which aimed to provide long-term unemployed with new skills. I met my husband, Jon, during this time and we moved to the Plymouth area with our jobs. Among other things I am a member of a local community choir who sing songs related to the environment and science composed by our choir leader – two of our many songs are appropriately called "Tree" and "Timber".

Autumn rain in Beaumont Park, Plymouth